DiG
3ft NW
THE LEGENDARY JOURNEY
OF BURKE & WiLLS

SARAH MURGATROYD

Text Publishing
Melbourne Australia

ILLUSTRATION SOURCES: Grateful acknowledgment is made to the following for permission to reproduce the illustrative material in the text: p. 3, p. 32, p. 44, p. 46, and p. 179 by William Strutt, Dixson Library, State Library of New South Wales; p. 77, p. 106, p. 144, and p. 206 from the La Trobe Australian Manuscripts Collection and La Trobe Picture Collection, State Library of Victoria; p. 22, Mortlock Library, State Library of South Australia; p. 207, National Library of Australia, Canberra.

The paper used in this book is manufactured only from wood grown in sustainable regrowth forests.

The Text Publishing Company
Swann House
22 William Street
Melbourne Victoria 3000
Australia
www.textpublishing.com.au

This is an abridged version of Sarah Murgatroyd's *The Dig Tree*, first published in 2002.

First published in Australia by The Text Publishing Company 2008
Printed and bound in Australia by Griffin Press
Designed by Chong
Typeset in Baskerville MT by J & M Typesetters
Maps by Tony Fankhauser

National Library of Australia Cataloguing-in-Publication data:
Murgatroyd, Sarah, 1967–2002.
Dig 3ft NW : the legendary journey of Burke and Wills / Sarah Murgatroyd.
Rev. ed.
Melbourne : The Text Publishing Company, 2008.
ISBN: 9781921351723 (pbk.)
For school age.
Burke and Wills Expedition 1860–1861. Australia--Discovery and exploration.
919.4043

This project has been assisted by the Commonwealth Government through the Australia Council, its arts funding and advisory body.

Sarah Murgatroyd was born in England in 1967 and grew up on a farm in Sussex. After a year in China, India and the Himalayas, she gained an honours degree in Philosophy and Literature at Warwick University, and then studied broadcast journalism at Cardiff University. In 1993 she came to Australia where she travelled extensively, providing news and current affairs coverage for the BBC. To research *The Dig Tree* she retraced the footsteps of Burke and Wills across Australia. Sarah died of cancer in March 2002, a few weeks after *The Dig Tree* was first published.

To Kevin

For winching me out of more creeks than I deserve

CONTENTS

This is one of the earliest known photographs of the Dig Tree. Taken around 1911, it shows the original message carved into the trunk and the remains of the stockade William Brahe built to protect the expedition's supplies.

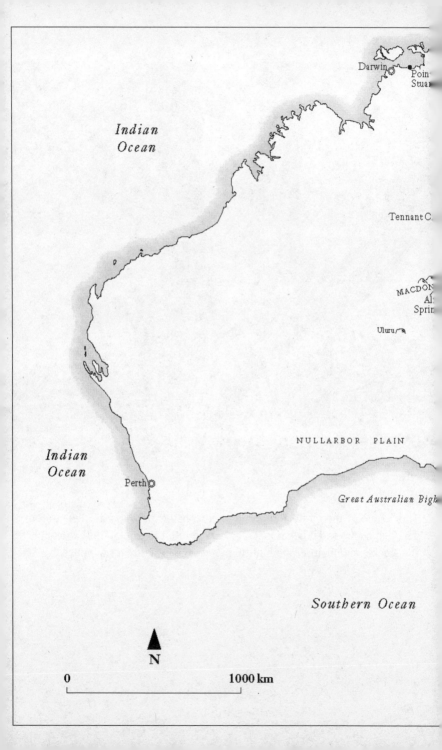

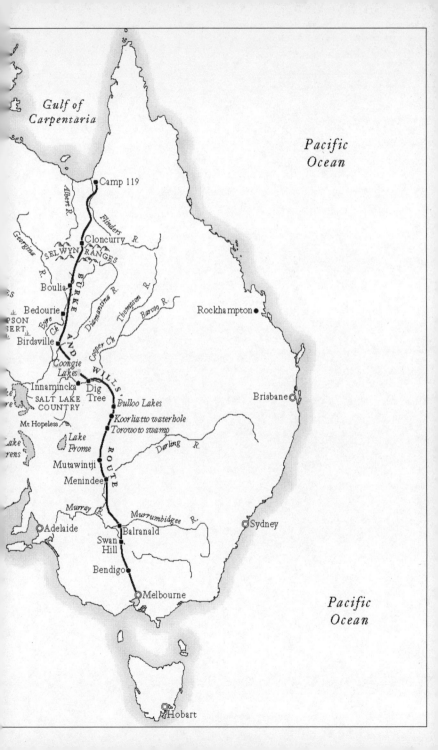

ONE

THE DEAD HEART

WHEN Captain James Cook stood on the deck of the *Endeavour* in 1770 and felt the hot dry winds off Australia's southern coast, he declared that the country's interior would be nothing but desert. Nearly a century later, as the sun rose, a small group of men emerged from the canvas tents pitched under the gum trees in Melbourne's Royal Park. The same hot wind blew in their faces and reminded them of the task ahead.

It was Monday 20 August 1860—the day the Victorian Exploring Expedition would set out to cross the driest inhabited continent on earth; an island the size of the United States of America, home to extraordinary creatures such as the kangaroo, the emu and the duck-billed platypus. The interior had confounded European settlers since their arrival in 1788. What else might lie hidden in a land that had rebuffed European explorers for so long?

Despite the early hour, crowds bustled towards the park expecting to see a highly organised operation. Instead, they found the expedition members rushing about, cursing under their breath as they tripped over the twenty tonnes of equipment scattered on the grass.

Many spectators made straight for the stables, intrigued by strange bellowing noises and peculiar smell. Those who managed to get inside saw four 'Indian' sepoys, wearing white robes and red turbans, trying to calm a small herd of camels that had been imported to conquer the deserts of central Australia. The animals were the pride of the expedition. They had each been fitted with a waterproof rug, complete with a hole for the hump, along with two sets of camel shoes, designed for travelling over stony ground. Even river crossings had been catered for. 'If it becomes necessary to swim the camels,' boasted the *Argus* newspaper, 'air bags are to be lashed under their jowls, so as to keep their heads clear when crossing deep streams.'

In the centre of the turmoil, standing on top of a wagon, was a tall flamboyant Irishman. Shouting orders in a strong Galway accent, expedition leader Robert O'Hara Burke was trying (and failing) to impose order on the mayhem below.

The Victorian Exploring Expedition had been organised by a committee of Melbourne's most important men. In July 1851 Victoria had severed ties with its parent colony of New South Wales and the expedition was designed to show off the achievements of a new and ambitious colony. Every eventuality was catered for. One 'hospital camel' was fitted with an enclosed stretcher. In order to cope with dry conditions, each man carried a 'pocket charcoal filter, by means of which he will be able to obtain drinkable water under the most unfavourable circumstances', and should anyone get lost, the party carried 'an abundance of signals, from the rocket and the blue light to the Union Jack and the Chinese gong'. The problem was—where to put it all?

By lunchtime the crowd had swelled to around 15,000, a good turnout for a city of 120,000. The expedition doctor, Hermann Beckler, recalled later, 'no member of the expedition

THE DEAD HEART

The only surviving photograph of the expedition leaving Royal Park shows Burke standing in the centre giving a speech to the city's dignitaries.

could see another…such was the crush among the thousands who thronged to see our departure'. A carnival atmosphere swept through the park. Whispers circulated that a 'sly grog shop' had opened up behind the camel stables.

By mid-afternoon an expedition member appeared 'a little too hilarious through excess of beer'. Burke had already dismissed two of his party for disobedience and he now fired ex-policeman Owen Cowan on the spot. The expedition was three men down— and it had not even finished packing.

One man avoided the revelry. Refusing to be interviewed, a neatly dressed young Englishman stayed inside his tent, wrapping his scientific instruments. Surveyor, astronomer, meteorologist and third-in-command, William John Wills packed his nautical almanacs, sextant, compass, theodolite, chronometer, barometer, thermometer, anemometer, telescope, sketchbooks, notebooks, specimen jars and bottles of preserving fluid. Wills was a born scientist. It was his mission to explain the world around him, and now at the age of twenty-six he had the opportunity to cross an entire continent, a journey he expected to last more than two years.

The expedition had been due to depart at one o'clock in the afternoon but 'hour after hour passed'. Burke was becoming flustered. With the city's dignitaries waiting to offer the official farewell, he was facing the embarrassing prospect of having to leave with only half his party. Impulsively, he hired two extra wagons and ordered that the rest of the supplies be loaded.

When the column of camels, horses and wagons finally assembled shortly before four o'clock, Burke addressed the crowd:

> On behalf of myself and the Expedition I beg to return you my most sincere thanks. No expedition has ever started under such favourable circumstances as this. The people, the government, the committee—they all have done heartily what they could do. It is now our turn; and we shall never do well till we justify what you have done in showing what we can do!

In private Burke was more forthright. 'I will cross Australia,' he told his friends, 'or perish in the attempt.'

The explorers began to march. Deputy leader George

Landells, who had responsibility for the camels, took the lead on an enormous bull camel, waving to the spectators. Burke followed on Billy, his favourite grey horse, and behind him stretched the procession, half a kilometre long.

Among the vehicles was a wagon designed so that 'it can be taken off the wheels, and put to all the uses of a river punt'. This revealed the explorers' uncertainty about what lay ahead. Some believed the Australian interior would reveal nothing more than a vast desert, others fantasised about mountain ranges, fertile plains, lost civilisations and wild animals unknown to science. A few believed there was an inland sea. The truth was—nobody knew.

Ahead lay a journey of at least 5000 kilometres, from the Southern Ocean to the Gulf of Carpentaria, the equivalent of marching from London to Moscow and back. As the speeches faded away, the magnitude of the task became apparent. Several of the wagons became bogged at the edge of the park. One broke down completely just beyond the camels' manure heap.

By the time Burke coaxed his expedition out of Melbourne in 1860, it was the age of overland exploration. Most of the world's great maritime voyages were over and every continent bar Antarctica was being poked, prodded and plundered by scientists, missionaries, traders and tyrants.

Australia revealed its secrets with reluctance. Unlike America, where the pioneers had spread out west as fast as their wagons could carry them, Australia's first colonies were convict settlements. The last thing the British government had in mind was a mass exploration of the country. In Sydney, the new immigrants spent the first few decades simply trying to survive, and when they felt secure enough to explore they found they were pinned to the east coast by the Blue Mountains.

Some convicts were convinced that China lay on the other side of the range, others told stories of fearsome warriors, savage kingdoms and dangerous animals. These myths were cultivated by the army to discourage escape attempts. But as conditions in Sydney improved and the fetters of convict society loosened, pioneers spilled north and south searching for new pastures and helped set up the cities of Melbourne, Adelaide and Brisbane.

Despite the opportunity to explore a landmass of 7.5 million square kilometres (about two-thirds the size of Europe), the new settlers showed a hesitancy to leave the coast. It seems strange that a new society could cling to the hemline of its adopted continent for so long—but with a small population and plenty of fertile soil, there was little incentive to travel inland.

As the towns grew into cities, people came to regard 'the bush' with a mixture of apathy and apprehension. According to settler John Sherer:

> There can be no walk, no journey of any kind, more mono-tonous than one through the bush…there is no association of the past connected with it…There are no sacred graves…no birthplaces of great men. Nothing of this kind; all is deadly dull, uninspiring hard work.

Early attempts to penetrate further inland were often made by farmers. They took off into the unknown, armed with little more than a rifle and ambition. Little by little, they extended their knowledge of the surrounding area, discovering grasslands and giant forests or stumbling over nuggets of gold. But eventually the coastal safety net gave way and the landscape became more menacing.

In 1858, a farmer known as Coulthard set out to find new pastures to Adelaide's north. His mummified body was later discovered by a government expedition. Before he died, he scratched a message into his empty water bottle:

> I never reached water…My Tung is stkig to my mouth and I see what I have wrote I know it is this is the last time I may have of expressing feeling alive & the feeling exu is lost for want of water My ey Dassels My tong burn. I can see no More God Help

It was only when politicians realised there was money to be made from new grazing lands that an assault on the inland began. Military-style expeditions of columns of horses and bullock carts were used to carry enormous quantities of supplies into the bush. After a hard day in the field, the officers would sit down at large oak tables in the middle of nowhere, to three-course dinners with silver cutlery, wine and spotless white napkins.

By the 1830s, the notoriously bad-tempered surveyor-general Sir Thomas Livingstone Mitchell was doing battle with New South Wales' river systems. Mitchell won recognition for opening up huge areas of grazing land in the far north-west of the colony, but when it came to unravelling the south-eastern rivers he faced a series of humiliating defeats.

Many of the waterways were boomerang-shaped, and had a bizarre tendency to curve inland and flow in the 'wrong' direction. This led Mitchell's great rival, Charles Sturt, to conclude that rivers like the Murray and the Murrumbidgee must eventually drain into an ocean in the middle of the continent. Why else, he reasoned, did seagulls mysteriously appear from the interior? Sturt was so confident that he pioneered the technique of building wagons that could be converted into small boats. With backing from the South Australian government, he set off from Adelaide in 1844, heading towards the centre of the continent.

It was a heartbreaking journey. The grass turned to rock and the cool winds of the coast were replaced by searing blasts of air slicing across the treeless plains. The waterholes dried up and the colour green vanished from the spectrum. At every turn he was confronted by vistas of sand, salt and clay. After 600 kilometres, his party became trapped between an expanse of white salt lakes and towering red dunes, 'the most forbidding that our eyes had wandered over'.

Tormented by mirages, Sturt continued north-west and became marooned in one of Australia's most unforgiving landscapes. After an agonising summer, entombed in a small rocky gorge, Sturt journeyed north. But his way was barred by 'gibber plains'—enormous expanses of bare earth covered in nothing but small purplish-red rocks. The area became known as Sturt's Stony Desert and it plagued Australian explorers for decades to come. As the stones sizzled in the sunlight, it was like crossing a giant barbecue. Within hours their boots were in tatters. The expedition's dog lost all the skin from its paws.

They were saved by a chain of waterholes lined with coolibah trees that seemed to appear from nowhere. The pools were linked by channels and formed a delicate ephemeral river system, known to the Aborigines as Kini-papa. Sturt named it Cooper's Creek after a South Australian judge.

It was only a temporary reprieve. Every time Sturt tried to leave the creek, the countryside reverted to a waterless wasteland.

A terrible drought gripped the country. It was one of the fiercest summers ever to be recorded. Even the local Aboriginal tribes were struggling to survive. There is no water, they told Sturt—'the sun has taken it'.

After months of torment, sick with scurvy and exhaustion, Sturt conceded defeat and turned south in November 1845. He abandoned his small wooden boat on the edge of the desert.

With so much of Australia unexplored, the continent proved irresistible to European scientists and adventurers. Ludwig Leichhardt, trained in zoology, botany, geography, geology and meteorology, arrived in 1841, determined to learn everything about his new environment. In 1846, Leichhardt led an expedition from Brisbane to the British settlement of Port Essington (north of the site of Darwin), across 4800 kilometres of largely uncharted territory. He returned to Sydney a hero but his glory was short-lived. His second expedition ended prematurely because of heavy rain. Undeterred, he set off again from Roma (to the west of Brisbane) in April 1848. It was a substantial party with seven men, fifty bullocks, 270 goats, seven horses, and tonnes of supplies—yet it vanished into the wilderness and was never seen again.

The New South Wales government asked surveyor Augustus Gregory to search for the lost scientist. Gregory was one of the first explorers to travel on horseback with a minimum of supplies. Between 1855 and 1858, he made a series of expeditions around the fringes of the central Australian deserts, but his efforts were frustrated by the lack of water. As Gregory explored the north-west of the continent, even major rivers like the Victoria splintered into thousands of rivulets and drained away.

9

Gregory's last hope of reaching the core of Australia was a watercourse he had named after Charles Sturt, but it too evaporated among the dunes. It was the final straw. Gregory gave up chasing the ghosts of lost scientists and invisible rivers—instead he decided to test a theory of his own.

In the 1840s, the explorer Edward Eyre had tried to penetrate the centre by travelling due north from Adelaide but he was thwarted by an impassable 'horseshoe' of salt lakes. Eyre's furthest point was a peak he named Mount Hopeless. Gregory was convinced that if he attacked the problem from the opposite direction, he could travel south down Cooper Creek, via Mount Hopeless to Adelaide, establishing a route from the heart of the desert back down to the coast.

The journey was difficult but Gregory emerged triumphant on the southern side of Mount Hopeless. It was the closest anyone had come to crossing the desert, but there was still about 1300 kilometres of unexplored country between the Cooper and the north coast of Australia. And Gregory's assessment of its potential was hardly enthusiastic:

> The universal character of the country along the boundary is level sandy desert or worthless scrub without any sign of change in advancing into the interior beyond that of increasing sterility…not one single stream emanates from this inhospitable region, to indicate ranges of hills, better soil or climate.

His reports fuelled the perception that the Australian interior was 'a scene of awful desolation, a sterile solitude, without a trace of verdure or a sign of life'.

Stories of Australia's 'dead heart' grew until the hellish descriptions seduced explorers, eager to tame such an impenetrable

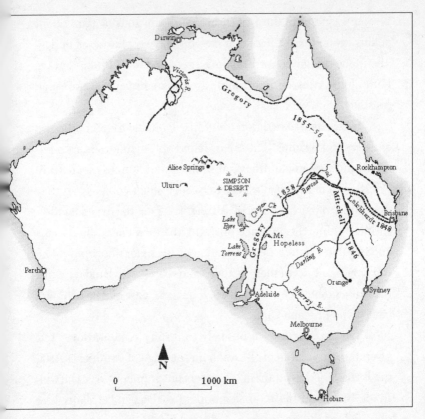

After Mitchell discovered the Barcoo River in 1846 and Leichhardt disappeared in 1848, Gregory forged a route through the deserts to Adelaide.

void. The catchcry 'There's nothing out there' started in the mid-nineteenth century, and the myth persists to this day.

It wasn't just the Australian deserts that repelled the European settlers. The northern regions had been as unpopular since the explorer William Dampier landed on the north-west coast in 1688 and reported that, 'The land is of a dry sandy soil, destitute of water.'

It wasn't until the British became suspicious of the French poking around in the area that they dispatched Matthew Flinders (the man who gave Australia its name), and later Phillip Parker King, John Wickham and John Stokes, to survey the northern coastline.

Each naval expedition found itself unable to penetrate the estuaries and swamps. The sailors found only 'mangroves, mosquitoes, mud and mosquitoes', and inhospitable natives. In 1839 Wickham sent two men ashore to fix their ship's compass. As they made their repairs, a party of Aborigines appeared, wielding their spears. With great presence of mind, the men folded their arms and began a vigorous demonstration of the sailor's hornpipe. The warriors threw down their weapons and roared with laughter while the sailors danced for their lives. The area, east of Darwin, was later named Escape Cliff.

These reports were unlikely to inspire colonisation—but given the area's strategic location on the edge of south-east Asia, the British tried to establish settlements near present-day Darwin. In the 1830s and 1840s, small groups of soldiers and civilians were dumped on the north coast, told to uphold the honour of the empire—and then left to fend for themselves. In the tropical heat, the new communities were soon strangled by fever. After visiting the settlement of Victoria on the Cobourg Peninsula in 1848, Thomas Huxley described it as, 'the most useless, miserable, ill-managed hole in Her Majesty's dominions'.

By 1860 nearly two-thirds of Australia remained unexplored. The desert remained oblivious to nearly a century of European colonisation. Its indigenous inhabitants lived and died as they had always done and, on the banks of Cooper Creek, stood the old coolibah trees, their roots responding to the floods and droughts that had dictated the rhythms of the interior for thousands of years. But the tranquillity would not last forever.

TWO

LIFTING THE VEIL

DR DAVID Wilkie was a distinguished doctor who had never ventured further than the odd country picnic. So it was somewhat surprising when, in 1857, he suggested that Victoria mount an expedition to search for Ludwig Leichhardt and unlock the secrets of Australia's enigmatic core.

At Melbourne's Philosophical Institute, Wilkie's plan was met with bewilderment. The members debated the idea and then responded as they would many times over the next three years. They formed a committee and ordered a report on the matter.

The Philosophical Institute, formed in 1855, was the sort of semi-social, semi-scientific organisation that sprang up among the educated classes throughout the British empire. Its members were a combination of professionals, self-taught amateurs, enthusiastic eccentrics or committed social climbers. The idea of a transcontinental expedition appealed to their sense of importance. Perhaps it was time for the infant colony of Victoria to prove itself.

Despite having thirty-two members, the new Exploration Committee, headed by Melbourne's mayor Dr Richard Eades, boasted just two men with experience in geographical discovery: the naturalist William Blandowski, who had led some small scientific collecting parties, and the government botanist Baron Ferdinand von Mueller, who had been with Augustus Gregory in northern Australia.

When Wilkie's plan was shown to Gregory, the explorer dismissed it as 'almost hopeless'. Mueller then suggested that a light party be sent out from Melbourne to the Darling River on a sort of apprenticeship journey for fledgling explorers. It could establish a depot just beyond the settled areas and the experience gained could be used to mount a more ambitious future expedition. This idea confused matters further and the Exploration Committee produced another long and inconclusive report.

At the next meeting, Mueller's report provoked a series of furious arguments. 'How could Victoria hope to cross the entire continent when it had no explorers and no one with any experience to lead the party?' shouted the institute's secretary John Macadam—doctor, pathologist, chemist and university lecturer. 'How many men would venture on a larger expedition until they had gained some experience on a smaller one?' 'Dozens! Dozens! Dozens!' screamed Blandowski. 'Two stockmen—yes, two stockmen, by Gott—would gallop across the whole distance and be back in five weeks!'

The discovery of gold gave Victoria the financial luxury to argue about exploration. In 1851, several large nuggets were found near Ballarat and then Bendigo, north-west of Melbourne.

The countryside was soon crawling with men headed towards the goldfields. By 1853 a thousand ships a year were arriving in Melbourne. Lieutenant-Governor La Trobe despaired as everyone headed for the hills. 'Cottages are deserted,' he complained, 'houses are to let, business is at a standstill, and even schools are closed. In some suburbs not a man is left.' The *Argus* couldn't resist poking fun, printing a mock dispatch from La Trobe to his colonial masters:

My Lord,

As nearly all my officers have 'sloped' for our extravagantly rich diggings, I am obliged to write my despatches with my own hand; besides having to clean my own boots, groom my horse, and do a little amateur wood chopping. I have no clerks and no constables. High and low are at Mt Alexander and, between ourselves, are doing more real work in a day than they used to spread comfortably enough over a month...

Yours, in a hurry, as I fear the chops are burning.

By the end of the 1850s gold had catapulted Melbourne from a primitive muddy port to the most magnificent colonial city in the southern hemisphere. Victoria's population jumped to half a million people. As Victoria's wealth spiralled, so did its scientific and cultural aspirations. The growing sophistication brought with it a shame that large portions of the continent were unmapped, unnamed and—to European eyes—unclaimed. Melburnians marvelled at aeronauts ascending to the skies in giant balloons, but no one could say for sure what lay between the city and the north coast.

The centre of Australia insulted the colonial mind; it refused to be parcelled up and tied down by lines of latitude and longitude. The newspapers called for a resumption of the colony's early enthusiasm for exploration.

Victoria, however, was the least likely of all the Australian territories to solve the continent's geographical conundrums. It was the smallest and southernmost mainland colony, hemmed in by New South Wales and South Australia. Despite no room for territorial expansion and little experience in exploration, Victoria's pride in its self-proclaimed status as 'the most advanced of the Australian sisterhood' fuelled the idea of a grand scientific enterprise.

The idea of a transcontinental expedition took root among Melbourne's elite. When the shouting died down at the Philosophical Institute meeting on 22 December 1857, it was decided that the project should be tackled with new resolve. The institute formed another Exploration Committee, this time with twenty-five members. Their job was to turn the rhetoric into reality.

The first requirement was money. Politicians were approached but refused. Then, in August 1858, an Irish businessman Ambrose Kyte stepped forward with an offer of £1000 towards an expedition, provided his fellow colonists subscribed at least another £2000. Victoria's chief justice and president of the Philosophical Institute, Sir William Stawell, tipped off the *Argus*, which announced the scoop the following morning. Suddenly the idea of crossing the continent didn't look so far-fetched after all.

The invention of the overland telegraph line also influenced Melbourne's Philosophical Institute. Australia remained dependent on Great Britain for government, goods, export markets and eligible young women. But there was a perpetual time lag since the ships took two to three months to bring news from Europe. Farmers had to wait almost a year before they discovered the price for last season's wool clip; settlers rushed home to visit a sick relative and found themselves in the nearest graveyard.

In 1844, the first cables were laid between Washington and Baltimore. Suddenly messages could be relayed over hundreds of kilometres with the click of a button. When engineers began to plan undersea cables, no corner of the globe seemed inaccessible.

By 1853, Britain could wield its influence through the copper wires as far afield as Germany, Austria, Russia and Turkey. Plans were under way to link America and Britain. When the Crimean War broke out in 1854, Australia realised how isolated it really was. Wild rumours circulated that the Russians were about to invade, and at the prospect of this rather unlikely offensive, calls mounted for a cable link to Europe.

An early suggestion called for the wire to go from south-east Asia all the way to Brisbane. The idea horrified the South Australians. Adelaide was the first port of call for the European clipper ships and the government made a good profit from disseminating the latest reports from around the globe to the other states. An east-coast telegraph line via Brisbane to Sydney would mean isolation and financial disaster. The governor of South Australia, Sir Richard MacDonnell commissioned a report which, unsurprisingly, stated that an overland route through the centre of the continent south to Adelaide was the most satisfactory option.

The undersea line via Brisbane never eventuated and a titanic struggle ensued between the warring factions. Western Australia wanted the telegraph line to come ashore in Albany on the south-west coast. Brisbane and New South Wales were adamant that the eastern option was preferable and Victoria wondered how it could secure the prize for itself. But while the overland route seemed the most logical solution, no one had actually travelled from one coast to the other—so who could say exactly where the telegraph should go?

The issue of the telegraph wire splintered Melbourne's Philosophical Institute into opposing factions. Scientists like Ferdinand

Mueller still envisaged a slow well-equipped expedition of distinguished scientists and artists to record the natural riches of the Australian interior. Politicians and businessmen such as Sir William Stawell were more concerned with controlling the telegraph line, and with the possibility of an overland trade route linking Melbourne with south-east Asia, and wanted a swift gallop across the continent to establish a suitable site for a northern port. Pastoralists wanted to find out if there was fertile soil in the centre of the continent that could be annexed to Victoria. They lobbied for a party led by an experienced bushman who knew decent pasture when he saw it.

Regardless of the shape the expedition would take, the Exploration Committee decided to import camels to help it transport supplies. This was seen as a strategic masterstroke that would give Victoria the advantage over other colonies whose explorers used horses and bullock carts. Editorial after editorial extolled their virtues. 'The camel, with a load of five to six hundred pounds upon its back,' the *Argus* enthused, 'will with the greatest facility proceed at a rate of forty or fifty miles, and if necessary, will go without water for a period of from ten to fourteen days…What might not be expected from an exploring party equipped with these ships of the desert?'

But the committee still had to raise the £2000 to supplement Kyte's offer. Despite rousing speeches on the value of exploration, most people did not want to pay for the privilege of finding out what lay in the centre of the continent.

The Philosophical Institute formed the Exploration Fund Committee, headed by Sir William Stawell. Ostensibly it was an independent body, yet all but one of its members also served on the Exploration Committee, leading to several farcical situations when one body had to 'resolve' a contentious issue with the other.

The *Herald* suggested that Victoria approach South Australia and New South Wales to propose 'a grand combined effort to complete the exploration of this continent'. But the South Australians, fearful of losing their monopoly on the overland telegraph, had been scathing since the expedition was first suggested and New South Wales was not interested. The Exploration Fund Committee meetings fell away from three times to once a week and by December 1858, they stopped altogether. The project seemed unlikely to survive the lethargy of a Melbourne summer, let alone the heat of the Australian desert.

It took the achievements of John McDouall Stuart to rouse the slumbering Victorians.

Stuart, a Scotsman who arrived in South Australia in January 1839, joined surveyor-general Charles Sturt's 1844 expedition towards the centre of Australia as a draughtsman. As the gruelling journey towards Cooper Creek took its toll, 'little Stuart' surprised everyone with his stamina and resourcefulness. He once saved the party by tracking a flock of pigeons to one of the few remaining waterholes in the area. Then, when the chief surveyor James Poole died from scurvy, Stuart took over, earning high praise from his leader.

The expedition with Charles Sturt cemented the desert landscape in Stuart's imagination. Throughout his life, Stuart was to return again and again to the Australian wilderness. He had the patience to endure the heat, dust and insects, and could look beyond its initial disguise of pallid uniformity to its intense transparent light and overpowering sense of space. The explorer Ernest Favenc understood this. 'Repellent as this country is,' he wrote, 'there is a wondrous fascination in it, in its strange loneliness, and the hidden mysteries it might contain, that call to the man who has known it.' Like many explorers Stuart was a social misfit, craving escape from the conventions of society and never comfortable with emotional commitment. Most of his friends were children or animals and he was so ill at ease staying in the city that he took to sleeping in the garden whenever possible.

In 1858 businessmen James and John Chambers and William Finke hired him to find agricultural land in and around the Flinders Ranges. Surveying new grazing runs allowed Stuart to spend most of his time in the bush, which was probably just as well as he drank whenever he went back to town. The son of one of Stuart's friends recalled:

> Oh, he is such a funny little man, he is always drunk. You won't be able to have him at your house. Papa couldn't. Do you know, once, when he got to one of Papa's stations, on coming off one of his long journeys, he shut himself up in a room, and was drunk for three days.

Next Finke and the Chambers brothers sent Stuart to disprove the 'Fertile Island Theory'—a prediction that the salt lakes Edward Eyre found around the north of the state would stifle any further terri-torial expansion, leaving South Australia isolated and enclosed by an impenetrable natural barricade. Stuart was delighted. It was the perfect opportunity to try out his new tactics for dealing with hostile country. His plan—to move as fast as possible with just a few horses—was risky but it would allow Stuart's party to cover ground more quickly.

An unusual portrait of John McDouall Stuart dressed in his 'exploring clothes'.

Stuart left the settled districts in June 1858 with an assistant, George Foster, and a young Aboriginal guide. The trio rode north towards the salt-lake country through the Flinders Ranges—soaring red escarpments and cavernous gorges stretching for 300 kilometres, before stopping in sheer rock walls that guard the desert beyond. To the north and west, there is nothing but brown earth and a string of sharp white salt lakes on the horizon.

This scorched landscape stretches all the way to Lake Eyre, a salt lake covering around 5800 square kilometres. Surrounded by the Tirari Desert, travellers through the ages have found the environment unsettling. The explorer Cecil Madigan wrote in 1940:

> There are other barren and silent places, but nowhere else is there such vast, obtrusive, and oppressing deadness…Death seems to stalk the land. The vast plain that is the lake is no longer a lake. It is the ghost of a lake, a horrible, white, and salt-crusted travesty.

Stuart rode north-west across the plains, searching for a mythical freshwater lake referred to by the Aborigines as Wingilpin. The northern settlers told stories of a giant oasis surrounded by gum trees and mobs of kangaroos—there were even rumours that the lost scientist Ludwig Leichhardt had been killed on its shores. Whenever Stuart asked the local tribes where the lake was, they would point in the direction he was heading (whatever that might be) and announce that it was 'five sleeps' away.

As the days passed, Stuart began to wonder if the lake was just wishful thinking. Everything was 'bleak, barren, and desolate'. But his persistence was rewarded by the discovery of a watercourse he named Chambers Creek. The party pushed on through good grazing country and it began to rain. Cracks in the drought-ravaged soil filled with water and overflowed until Stuart found himself 'on an island before we knew what we were about.' The next day the floods receded and the men made for drier ground, crossing a small range of mountains. On the other side, the whole world turned white.

Stuart had stumbled onto the bleached stony plains that surround the present-day opal mines of Coober Pedy—an alien landscape since used in science fiction movies. The town's name comes from the Arabana Aboriginal term *kupa piti*, which means 'white man's hole'. As he rode through the bleak landscape, Stuart found that the intense light reflecting off the white rocks caused constant mirages. They were so powerful, he wrote, 'that little bushes appear like great gum-trees, which makes it very difficult to judge what is before us; it is almost as bad as travelling in the dark'. With no sign of better country ahead, the explorers were in a precarious position. They had been away for more than two months. The horses were lame, game was scarce and their supplies were almost gone. On 16 July 1858 Stuart swung southwards—he couldn't 'face the stones again'.

The retreat came just in time. They were down to their last loaf of damper when they noticed the first signs of fertility returning to the countryside. Seizing his chance to escape, the Aboriginal guide deserted Stuart and Foster. The ragged pair trudged towards the Nullarbor Plain and once more the country-side degenerated into a 'dreary, dismal, dreadful desert'. 'When will it end?' asked Stuart in his journal.

It was five agonising days before Stuart spotted fresh horse tracks in sand, an indication he was nearing the south coast. From an old hand-drawn map, he judged that they would reach water

Stuart kept to a similar route on his three attempts to cross the continent. His discovery of mound springs between the Flinders Ranges and Oodnadatta helped him reach central Australia.

the next day. Twenty kilometres later the men stumbled into Millers Water, near Ceduna on the Great Australian Bight, as Stuart had predicted. They were safe.

His journey was an outstanding achievement. He had travelled through more than 1600 kilometres of inhospitable territory using only a compass to navigate and he had mapped out thousands of square kilometres of potential sheep country. The total cost of his journey was £10 for food and £28 for his assistant's wages. The expedition completed Stuart's rigorous apprenticeship. He had been out with one of Australia's greatest explorers, he had honed his bush skills through years of surveying and now, he had completed a major journey with minimal equipment. More than most European men alive, he had come to terms with the capriciousness of the Australian desert.

Stuart seemed oblivious to the desert's detrimental effect on his health. As he travelled home to tell his patrons of his discoveries, he called in to see his fellow Scotsman, Robert Bruce, the manager of Arkaba Station. Bruce recalled:

> I turned to see a pallid pasty-faced looking face, crossed by a heavy moustache, and roofed in with a dirty cabbage tree hat, peering through the rails. 'You have the advantage of me,' said I, though the man's voice sounded very familiar to my ears. 'Oh, you know me all right, I'm Mr Stuart,' he responded... 'I thought I knew your voice,' I replied politely, 'but what have you been doing with yourself? Your voice is all that is left of you.'

During 1859 Stuart and three men explored the northern end of Lake Eyre and discovered a chain of mound springs running for hundreds of kilometres through some of the most barren areas on the continent. This ready supply of fresh water was the key to breaking through the horseshoe of salt lakes. The geological fault line led Stuart to rivers that beckoned towards the interior. Now more than ever he was determined to 'lift the veil' that hung over central Australia, and cross the continent from coast to coast.

THREE

MEETING BURKE

WHEN Stuart returned to Adelaide in July 1859, South Australia's politicians were delighted. Stuart had proved that fertile land lay beyond the salt lakes, and strengthened the case for bringing the overland telegraph line down to Adelaide.

William Finke and James Chambers offered to make Stuart available for an attempt to cross the continent. Their terms were simple: the government would have to cover part of the cost and offer a bonus for reaching the north coast. The South Australian governor was enthusiastic but the treasurer was unsure. He was eager for glory but reluctant to pay for it. Perhaps, he suggested, New South Wales and Victoria might like to contribute?

Both states declined, Victoria not very politely. Months of Adelaide newspaper editorials, pouring scorn on their exploratory efforts, had fuelled their determination to mount their own expedition.

South Australia switched tactics. In August 1859 it announced a prize of £2000 for the 'first person who shall succeed in crossing through the country lately discovered by Mr Stuart, to either the north or north-western shore of the Australian continent, west of the 143rd degree of east longitude'. This was a crafty ploy to induce the Victorians to plan their route for South Australia's benefit. The prize required them to travel through the territory that Adelaide needed to open up for the overland telegraph.

The prize jolted Melbourne's Philosophical Institute into action. Exploration Committee meetings resumed with renewed enthusiasm, but now the original scientific intentions were replaced by politics, intercolonial rivalry and greed. It had become a race between South Australia and Victoria—with £2000 waiting for the winner. The *Argus* predicted that Stuart would win the race before Victoria had even saddled its camels.

Talk of northern ports, pastoral land and the telegraph line, made Victoria's new chief secretary William Nicholson realise the proposed expedition offered more than a couple of new flower species—parliament allocated £6000 for the exploration. Shortly afterwards the Philosophical Institute was granted a royal charter and became the Royal Society of Victoria.

On 23 January, the Exploration Fund Committee dissolved itself and the Exploration Committee slimmed down to seventeen, including Ferdinand Mueller, John Macadam, geologist Alfred Selwyn, Sir William Stawell, the surveyor-general Charles Ligar, and pastoralist Angus MacMillan. Stawell was appointed chairman. There were still only three men (Mueller, MacMillan and Selwyn) who had any experience of exploration. With only this shallow pool of expertise to draw upon, the committee began to choose an expedition leader.

There weren't many suitable candidates. Thomas Mitchell had retired. Charles Sturt had returned to England and Ludwig Leichhardt had disappeared. Augustus Gregory was the obvious choice but he had accepted an offer from Queensland to become its new surveyor-general.

The naturalist William Blandowski put his own name forward. But a few months earlier he had settled a few personal scores by naming grotesque species of fish after particular members of the Royal Society. When the names were published, Blandowski realised his career was unlikely to progress much further. He sailed to Europe soon afterwards.

Ferdinand Mueller was unwilling to lead the expedition himself but had a candidate in mind: Major Peter Egerton Warburton, South Australian police commissioner and ex-army officer. In 1857, Warburton was dispatched to recover a surveying team and made valuable discoveries of fertile country north of Adelaide. Several committee members supported his candidacy, including Mueller and the prominent artist and naturalist Ludwig Becker. But the rest of the Royal Society refused to endorse Warburton because the Major disliked working with camels and because he was South Australian. The idea of a 'crow-eater' in charge of a Victorian expedition was unthinkable, particularly to William Nicholson. To Mueller's dismay, Warburton was sidelined. Then in a bizarre departure from protocol, the committee advertised the job of 'Expedition Leader'. The *Herald* was appalled. 'Men of science, of enterprise, and with some knowledge of the ways of the world,' it exclaimed, 'do not relish the notion of being advertised for, as the keeper of a registry office advertises for a butler, housemaid or a cook.'

Of the fifteen respondents, only four had any experience of adventurous travel but none had led a major expedition. The others ranged from dreamers and lunatics to armchair travellers and military men. Warburton refused to respond at all.

Pummelled by scathing newspaper editorials and public dissatisfaction, the Exploration Committee sank further into indecision. Reports of drunkenness and factional infighting at meetings were leaked to the press and by March 1860 the situation was desperate.

While the Victorians bickered, news arrived from South Australia that John McDouall Stuart had set out with two men from Chambers Creek. If there was to be a race, it seemed that one side had already started.

On 8 March, the *Argus* warned that the expedition was in danger of collapse. 'The exploration committee are in an embarrassing position. Time presses. The season of the year in which the expedition should set out is rapidly passing away, the camels have not yet arrived; no leader has been appointed.' A sub-committee drew up a shortlist of possible leaders including most people who had applied for the post—plus Warburton, who hadn't submitted his name at all.

Among the candidates was a police superintendent from Castlemaine and Beechworth, Robert O'Hara Burke. Although there is no record of a personal application, Burke's name was put forward by a senior officer, P. H. Smithe, who assured the committee Burke was:

> a most active man and very strong—most temperate in his habits—and is kind and gentler in his manners—but possessing a strong will—ambitious and had been accustomed to command since boyhood.

It was said that Burke had powerful backers within the Royal Society but, with no previous experience, he was initially passed over in favour of Gustav von Tempsky, who had 'drilled and fought Indians, Blacks, White and Redskins' during his thirteen years in America. He was questioned at length by the committee. A report was prepared. No decision was made.

Then the committee made an announcement—it had decided not to make any further decisions for another three months as the camels had not yet arrived and all the remaining applicants were to be given three months to learn the art of 'taking lunars'—that is, navigating by the stars. The committee was admitting that not one of their otherwise 'suitable' candidates could find his way home through the bush. By now, most of Melbourne was convinced that the selection process was rigged; a candidate had been promised the appointment and he was being given time to brush up on his navigational skills.

The camels arrived on 16 June 1860. By this time, John McDouall Stuart had been heading north for nearly four months. The *Register* couldn't resist a dig at its neighbour:

> It is quite possible and by no means improbable that at this moment the problem of the interior is solved and that John McDouall Stuart will be back in time to show the camels a beaten track through the heart of the Australian mainland.

With the camels ready to go, there was no excuse to delay appointing a leader. The impasse was broken at a meeting on 20 June 1860. The three candidates left in the race were Warburton (despite the fact he had not applied), Gustav von Tempsky and Robert O'Hara Burke.

Warburton's principal supporter, Ferdinand Mueller was sick and stayed away and several other committee members boycotted the meeting. As a result, discussions centred on von Tempsky and Burke. When the last vote was taken, no one supported Warburton and just five committee members chose von Tempsky. The clear winner with ten votes was Police Superintendent Robert O'Hara Burke.

Burke presented this portrait to Julia Mathews, whom he first met in 1858, when he proposed to her for the final time.

The Victorian Exploring Expedition finally had a leader—a man who had never travelled beyond the settled districts of Australia, who had no experience of exploration and who was notorious for getting lost on his way home from the pub.

Newspapers greeted Burke's appointment with a mixture of relief and incredulity. Most commentators were pleased that a

Victorian candidate had triumphed, but others were baffled. Did the policeman possess any relevant qualifications for the post?

Until recently Burke had been unknown in Melbourne society but reporters soon discovered he had an intriguing past. He was born in Ireland in 1820, the second son of a distinguished family. At the age of twenty, Burke became a cadet in the military, and by 1847 he had been promoted twice and was posted to Italy. Life in the regiment was tough but the army also had its perks. Once on leave, Burke travelled to the great European cities and, dressed in the uniform of his elite regiment, found that doors opened into a glamorous world.

The young Irishman hunted, gambled, and chased women— all the things expected of a young officer. He was intelligent, musical, well-read, and could flatter anyone he chose in French, Italian and German. With another promotion at the end of 1847, he seemed to be on the brink of a glittering career. Yet just a few months later he was facing ruin at the hands of a military court.

As his regiment prepared for action in Sardinia, Burke went absent without leave. Rumours circulated that he was ill with constipation but it seems more likely that he was escaping a mountain of gambling debts.

By the time he returned to his regiment early in 1848, he was facing a court martial and possibly jail. Fortunately, an inquiry found he had run up his debts through 'carelessness' rather than deceit. Burke was allowed to resign—his punishment was the dishonour of a shattered reputation.

Burke then turned to the police force and joined the Irish Constabulary in County Kildare. He quickly made a name for himself but found the life of a country policeman monotonous and the salary inadequate. A transfer to Dublin's mounted police failed to curb his restlessness. He hung around in the city's bars, where stories of gold and adventure in Australia cut through the haze of tobacco smoke and fired his imagination. As a member of the gentry, he was more fortunate than most—family connections gave him strings to pull, and Burke accumulated a portfolio of references from men who barely knew him, but proclaimed he was 'a man with unusual and extensive knowledge of the world'. Thus armed, he set sail for Australia.

By the time he landed in Melbourne in 1853, Victoria's gold rush was in full swing and the colony was in desperate need of police officers. So many fortune seekers had arrived that most miners were struggling to make a living and Burke soon realised that gold mining was not the guaranteed route to wealth he had imagined. He fell back into a police career and was made an acting inspector at Beechworth, 260 kilometres north-east of Melbourne.

The position was not an easy one. Crime was rife and ethnic disagreements between the European and Chinese immigrants created unease in the valleys. Bushrangers menaced the highways (the Kelly gang would terrorise the area in the late 1870s), cattle rustlers stalked the plains and petty thieves harassed the shopkeepers. The pubs were crawling with diggers drowning their sorrows or picking fights. Or both.

For Burke, life in Australia was proving to be depressingly similar to the one he had left behind in Ireland. The only compensation was the salary. At £700 a year, it was three times what he would have made back home.

Away from the bright lights of Europe, Burke ceased to maintain his image. Despite his rank, Burke did not appear to possess a full police uniform and he was known to rush around borrowing clothing from his colleagues whenever a local dignitary was due in town. On or off duty, he didn't care what he looked like, and was often seen wearing check trousers, a red shirt and a threadbare jacket covered in patches. Underneath a peculiar sombrero-type hat, his hair was unkempt and his face obscured by a black beard, over which he was sometimes said to dribble saliva.

But the real gossip centred on Burke's bathing habits. Neighbours whispered he was 'as fond of water as a retriever', and that he often spent hours lying in his outdoor bathtub, wearing nothing but his police helmet, reading a book and cursing the mosquitoes. Several people wondered if he was perhaps 'a trifle insane'.

Despite this Burke was popular and capable. He had a knack for imposing strict discipline yet remaining friendly with his subordinates. He became famous for his tales of adventure in Europe and was so well-liked that, when he later applied for a transfer to the town of Castlemaine, the residents of Beechworth petitioned him to stay on.

Then, in 1854, Burke's younger brother James became the first British officer to be killed in the Crimean war. Burke was profoundly affected by the glorious (if exaggerated) account of his brother's death reported in the *Age*. The tragedy continued to weigh on his mind, so in March 1856 he left to join the British army. He arrived in Liverpool to find his services were not required. The fighting was over and a peace treaty had already been signed.

Disappointed, Burke returned to Australia and by the end of 1856 he was back in his old position at Beechworth. With the gold now beginning to run out, the only real excitement was a riot staged by European and American miners trying to drive the Chinese away from the diggings. At gunpoint, they herded the Chinese miners like sheep until some fell down a gorge into the Buckland River. When Burke heard of the trouble, he took twenty men and rode the eighty kilometres to Buckland in just twenty-four hours. As they neared the scene, there was talk of an ambush but Burke refused to turn back. Placing himself in front of his men, he charged into the miners' camp—only to find it deserted. The unrest was over. Just as he had missed the height of the gold rush and the fighting in the Crimea, Burke turned up at Buckland too late to take part in the real action. It seemed he had a talent for bad timing.

In 1858, a travelling theatre company came to town. Its star performer was Julia Mathews, a sixteen-year-old actress described by the critics as 'sparkling, gay and bewitching'. Burke went to see Julia perform, and fell uncontrollably in love with her. On her last night he went backstage and asked her to marry him. Even by Burke's standards, it was an outrageous proposal. He was a thirty-eight-year-old Protestant police officer and she was a Catholic actress (a disreputable profession in those days) less than half his age.

The offer horrified Julia's mother. Her daughter was already earning the vast sum of £60 per week (of which Julia received just 2s 6d) and Mrs Mathews envisaged a long and lucrative career, not an early wedding to a country police officer. But her opposition could not deter Burke. On the pretext of tracking a gang of dangerous horse thieves, Burke spent the next few weeks charging around Victoria to watch Julia perform. Julia may have

Julia Mathews was a seductive actress and singer who captivated Burke until he was prepared to risk everything to win her love.

been susceptible, but all the Irish charm in the world could not persuade her mother, who took her daughter back to Melbourne. Burke returned to Beechworth.

In the weeks that followed, neighbours noticed that his cottage was filled with music. He had bought a piano and was playing out his grief through Julia's songs. Later, when the heartbroken policeman remembered that his next-door neighbour was expecting a baby, he draped blankets over the piano to dampen the noise. When the baby was delivered, Burke told the father, with tears in his eyes: 'Ah, if I had such ties as you have, I think I should be a happier and better man.'

The Irishman's life had stalled. In November 1858, he transferred to the larger Castlemaine district, where along with two hundred others from the town, he subscribed two shillings and sixpence to the 'Exploration Fund'—little knowing that one day he would be leading the expedition.

The opportunity to escape presented itself with the arrival of a railway tycoon named John Bruce—a businessman who often used the local police to quell disturbances staged by his disgruntled workers. The two men became friends and Bruce smartened up his protégé and introduced him to the 'right people' in Melbourne. When the Royal Society announced it was looking for an expedition leader, Bruce encouraged Burke to apply.

The idea of Burke leading any expedition anywhere at all was ludicrous. He was neither a surveyor nor a scientist and had no exploration experience. His talent for getting lost was legendary. His bank manager, Falconer Larkworthy, observed:

It was said of him as a good joke but true nevertheless, that when he was returning from Yackandandah to Beechworth he lost his way, although the track was well beaten and frequented, and did not arrive at his destination for many hours after he was due. He was in no sense a bushman.

Beechworth's police officers often had to retrieve their chief from 'his latest confusion' and the *Mount Alexander Mail* revealed, 'he could not tell the north from the south in broad daylight, and the Southern Cross as a guide was a never ending puzzle to him'. How would he cope in the wilderness with no roads or signposts? How could he travel in a straight line when he couldn't even measure latitude and longitude?

So why was such an unlikely candidate chosen to lead the most prestigious project Victoria had ever undertaken?

Many commentators accepted Burke's appointment because he came from an ancient and honourable family and was 'accustomed to command'. Never mind that he could hardly read a compass—he had the right blood flowing through his veins.

One reporter was impressed with Burke's physical attributes. 'He was tall, well-made with dark brown hair; his broad chest was decorated with a magnificent beard; he had fine intelligent eyes, and a splendidly formed head.' Then there was Burke's dashing history and his mysterious scar, all of which appealed to the ladies of Melbourne. The chief justice's wife Mary Stawell gushed:

> When we first met Mr Burke we called him 'Brian Boru'; there was such a daring reckless look about him which was enhanced by a giant scar across his face, caused by a sabre cut in a duel when he was in the Austrian service.

In 1859 Burke had joined the Melbourne Club, allowing him access to the rich and powerful including men like Sir William Stawell, who was as impressed by Burke as his wife had been.

As the leadership battle dragged on through April and May of 1860, Gustav von Tempsky embarked on a rigorous training program. Burke took a rather different approach. He was normally to be found in the bar of the Melbourne Club losing money at cards but winning plenty of friends. At times his debts reached up to £450—nearly two-thirds of his annual salary.

As Burke's losses mounted, John Bruce and his associates manipulated matters in the background, leaning on friends, calling in favours, even conspiring to stack the Exploration Committee with members sympathetic to the cause. Their most important conquest was Sir William Stawell. Once he supported Burke, several committee members including Professor Georg Neumayer and John Macadam followed suit.

Burke enjoyed every minute in the limelight. Perhaps in his more romantic moments he imagined himself like the knights of old—he had been given a quest, a chance to prove himself and perhaps to secure the woman he loved. In the meantime he set about getting fit. Reports began to appear in the newspapers of a red-faced man jogging around Melbourne's Royal Park. It was Burke, tackling 'the severest of physical privations' to ready himself for the journey ahead.

On 4 July 1860 a ragtag assortment of prospective explorers queued outside the headquarters of the Royal Society. Seven hundred men applied to join the venture. Many men offered to go for minimal wages; some said they would go for none at all.

The inspection process was a charade. Burke spent just three hours looking at three hundred of the applicants then dismissed them all in favour of men with the 'right' connections. He ignored candidates like Robert Bowman and William Weddell, who had travelled with Augustus Gregory.

Twenty-five-year-old William Brahe was chosen largely because his brother was a friend of Georg Neumayer. John Macadam recommended sailor Henry Creber as a useful man in case an inland sea was discovered. Robert Fletcher's father was a friend of several committee members. Blacksmith William Patten and labourer Thomas McDonough knew Burke back in Ireland, Patrick Langan met him in Castlemaine and Owen Cowan was a fellow Victorian police officer.

Once the men had been chosen, the Exploration Committee decided that the expedition should leave by the end of August 1860. The Exploration Committee issued Burke's official instructions, which started clearly enough—Burke would form a base, a depot of provisions and stores at Coopers Creek, and open a line of communication from there with the Committee.

After that, however, the orders became vague and confused. Burke was to explore the country between Coopers Creek and Leichhardt's track, south of the Gulf of Carpentaria, avoiding Sturt's route to the west and Gregory's to the east. If this wasn't possible he was to turn west into the country recently traversed by Stuart, and connect his further point northward with Gregory's furthest Southern Exploration in 1856 (Mount Wilson). If Burke failed to connect the two points, or if they had already been traversed he was to connect his exploration 'with those of the younger Gregory in the vicinity of Mount Gould, and thence… proceed to Shark's Bay, or down the River Murchison to the settlements in Western Australia.'

The instructions effectively allowed Burke to go wherever he chose. The next paragraph admitted as much:

> The Committee is fully aware of the difficulty of the country you are called on to traverse, and in giving you these instructions has placed these routes before you more as an indication of what is deemed desirable to have accomplished than as indicating any exact course for you to pursue.

These orders only reinforced the growing sentiment that the Exploration Committee was not capable of organising a Sunday picnic. The rumours surrounding Burke's appointment had intensified until he was forced to defend himself, insisting he had used 'only fair and honourable means' to secure his position. But the *Age* still suspected the public was not being told the whole story:

> If Mr B's scientific attainments are equal to the task, let the public know them, if they are not, the public will protest against a piece of cliqueism in which the interests of the country are again sacrificed to please and serve the purposes of an unscrupulous and dangerous party.

Some columnists predicted that the expedition would be a disaster. One forecast that lives would be lost.

FOUR

DAY ONE

ON its first day, the Victorian Exploring Expedition with its twenty-six camels, twenty-three horses, nineteen men and six wagons travelled just eleven kilometres. It was seven-thirty in the evening on 20 August 1860 before the cavalcade straggled into Essendon on the outskirts of Melbourne. The camels stood incongruously on the green in front of the church and, smelling their arrival, all the local horses promptly bolted.

The laborious business of unpacking then began. No one knew where anything was, who was responsible for what, or how the camp should be organised. To compound matters, the wagons still hadn't arrived. Even Burke was not sure what was going on. He marched around the camp, telling his men that if he found anyone guilty of disobedience or idleness 'he would nail the culprit up by the ears to the nearest gum tree'.

As the Irishman tried to impose order, an elderly man approached him. It was Dr Wills—the father of the expedition's young surveyor, William John Wills. Grasping Burke's hand, the doctor launched into a plea for his son's safety. 'If it were in my power, I would even now prevent his going…If he knew what I am about to say, he would not, I think be well pleased; but if you ever happen to want my son's advice or opinion you must ask it, for he will not offer it unasked. No matter what course you may adopt he will follow without remonstrance or murmur.'

The chaotic first night's camp at Essendon. Burke is in the centre in his cabbage-tree hat. Landells is just to the left of him. Becker stands in front of the tent.

'There is nothing you can say will raise him higher in my estimation than he stands at present,' Burke replied. 'I will do as you desire.' With tears in his eyes, the doctor turned away.

Since neither the leader nor the deputy could navigate, twenty-six-year-old William Wills held an unusually important position, but as the protégé of Professor Georg Neumayer, his appointment was proposed and seconded without debate.

Wills was born in Totnes, Devon, in 1834. Nicknamed 'Old Jack' or 'Gentleman Jack' as a child because of his serious outlook on life, he contracted 'remittent fever' at the age of seven and suffered afterwards from a slight speech impediment. Always precocious, Wills spent his spare time helping out at his father's medical practice. 'In all cases his caution was extreme,' wrote Dr Wills senior, '…The ordinary operations of extracting a tooth, or breathing a vein when a bumpkin presented himself as a patient, he speedily mastered.'

At seventeen Wills went to London where he demonstrated his extraordinary sense of direction by unravelling London's Hampton Court maze in less than ten minutes. Friends described him as a serious, unassuming young man whose affable manner belied his strong opinions. Wills had intended to study as a surgeon but he was never truly enthusiastic about medicine and soon turned to the purer sciences of maths, geometry and physics, where he excelled in every subject.

The lure of gold drew the Wills family to Australia. William and his younger brother Tom sailed for Melbourne in 1852, ahead of their father, arriving in January 1853 at the pinnacle of the gold rush. They were shocked by the exorbitant prices and the shortage of accommodation. Nineteen-year-old Wills was not impressed with Melbourne and he and Tom found work as shepherds near the town of Deniliquin just over 250 kilometres away. After a three-week walk to start work, the brothers soon settled in and seemed to relish their new lifestyle. Wills told his family:

> We are very comfortable in a hut by ourselves…with between 13 or 14 hundred rams to look after…We are very well off in the way of food; as much mutton as we like and we can make

sure of getting a duck, pigeon or cockatoo at any time almost without going out of sight of the hut, besides plenty of fish in the creek. There are also plenty of mussel fish.

He got to know the landscape, the animals, birds, and even the finer points of sheep farming. It wasn't long before the Australian bush had captured his imagination:

Engrossed by his scientific studies, Wills was unaware of the public interest in the expedition and reluctant to pose for an official portrait.

If you had only let us come out without a shilling it would have been worth more than a thousand pounds in England, one is so free. This is a beautiful country, the more I see of it the better I like it.

In August 1853, Dr Wills joined his sons and took them to the gold-mining town of Ballarat, where he set up a surgery amongst the wooden shacks and maze of muddy trenches. Wills junior started a successful business analysing specimens of quartz and gold but his father recalled that 'he was ever pining for the bush…the study of nature was his passion. His love was fixed on animals, plants, and the starry firmament.'

Wills soon began to dream of exploring further afield. In 1855 he walked 160 kilometres in the hope of joining an expedition led by a Dr Catherwood. Before he left he told his mother not to worry about the dangers because, 'if everyone had such ideas we should have no one going to sea for fear of being drowned, no one would go in a railway train for fear the engine would burst, and all would live in the open air for fear of houses falling in'. The expedition was a fraud. By the time Wills caught up to him, Dr Catherwood had bolted, taking with him several hundred pounds in public subscriptions.

In 1856 Wills found work as a junior surveyor measuring out new leases, but science was still his major obsession. Wills' studies convinced him that it was science, not God, which would explain the universe and everything that happened within it. In 1858, the head of Melbourne's new Flagstaff Observatory, Professor Georg Neumayer, offered him a post as an assistant.

Wills was thrilled, two years later, when he discovered he had been chosen as the expedition's 'Surveyor and Astronomical

Observer'. He told his mother:

> The actual danger is nothing, and the positive advantages very great…Were we born, think you, to be locked up in comfortable rooms, and never to incur the hazard of mishap? If things were at the worst, I trust I could meet death with as much resignation as others, even if it came tonight.

His professional colleagues knew him to be an intelligent, dependable, abstemious young man with a talent for surveying and a strong sense of duty. Without realising it, the Exploration Committee had chosen the perfect foil for Robert O'Hara Burke.

On the day of departure, Wills spent several hours ensuring his equipment was properly loaded and arrived in Essendon a few hours later to find that Burke had already disappeared. His deputy George Landells was in charge of the camp. Landells shouted orders in his strong Northumberland accent and fussed around the camels. As well as the precious imported animals, Landells was also in charge of six other camels, purchased by the Exploration Committee on the spur of the moment for £50 from local circus impresario George Coppin. Untrained and undersized, they were already proving a hindrance to the smooth running of the expedition.

Landells had been a popular choice as deputy leader. As soon as the camels arrived he had become quite a celebrity, impressing everyone including Burke with his mastery of the animals and his ability to communicate with the Indian sepoys. Aware of his value, Landells played hard to get. He submitted a long list of conditions to the Exploration Committee. These included a £600 salary and a guarantee that he would be in charge of all matters relating to the camels. In addition the expedition would have to carry 270 litres of rum for the camels for 'medicinal purposes'.

The committee was in a difficult position. Landells had asked for a salary £100 a year greater than Burke's and by insisting on full control of the camels he was undermining the authority of the expedition leader. Burke continued to support Landells and, in a dramatic gesture, he refused to allow the committee to increase his own salary to £600 as well. Under increasing pressure to appoint someone, the Exploration Committee capitulated to Landells' financial demands and, although they could not officially grant him authority over the camels, they told the Englishman in private that where the management of the animals was concerned he could expect Burke to follow his advice without question. In doing so, the committee implicitly admitted that Burke was incapable of commanding all aspects of the enterprise. It broke the cardinal rule of 'one ship, one captain' and placed the two inexperienced, highly strung men on a collision course from the beginning.

Using Landells to import camels to Victoria may have been a daring move by the Royal Society but their introduction came at a cost. Landells had spent double his budget and arrived back in Melbourne seven months later than planned. The delay meant that the expedition had missed the cool winter season between April and September.

But Landells reassured the committee that his camels could perform in any climate. The committee went along with his advice. In its haste to beat Stuart it ignored the wisdom of all Australia's most experienced explorers and ordered the expedition to leave during the height of summer. Burke had neither the knowledge nor the patience to resist.

Landells brought six men with him on the expedition. The first, John Drakeford, was to serve as a camel handler and cook. He had worked in Africa and claimed that he could have explored with Livingstone but 'chose not to'. The second man, John King, was a small shy character, who had been discharged from the army in India for 'fever of a bad type'. No one was quite sure if he had completely recovered.

The other four were 'sepoy' camel handlers. Their exact origin and religion is confused by the fact that they were often classified as simply 'Indians' or 'Afghans', but the expedition's artist Ludwig Becker described Samla as a Hindu, Dost Mohomet and Esau Khan as Muslims, and Belooch as a Parsee. They were paid two shillings a week—less than a third of the wages of the other men.

It was late in the evening before the first of the wagons rolled into Essendon. Much of the gear that had been loaded just a few hours earlier now had to be unpacked all over again. Men grappled with unfamiliar equipment, struggled with unruly animals and discovered that everything took longer than they had anticipated. As darkness settled around the campsite, John Drakeford prepared supper. Soon large metal pots bubbled over campfires and the men began to line up with their tin plates and mugs.

Charles Ferguson was the camp supervisor. Officers were not expected to trouble themselves with day-to-day matters, so a reliable foreman was required. But 'rogue' might have been a more appropriate description.

Ferguson was an American from Ohio. He had fought and plundered his way through the Californian goldfields before chasing his dreams to the diggings in Victoria. When Australia's most famous rebellion broke out at Eureka in 1854 as the miners revolted over the cost of their licences, Ferguson found himself being arrested and handcuffed to one of the ringleaders, Raffaello Carboni. Once he had talked his way out of the resulting criminal charges, Ferguson went on to dabble in cattle trading and horse breaking.

Ferguson was in the goldfields of Kiandra in New South Wales when he heard of the expedition. It is unclear just how he came to join the party. By his own account, he was so essential to the operation that both the Exploration Committee and Burke invited him. After bargaining hard over his pay, he signed up as foreman on a salary of £200 per annum. Not everyone was impressed with Ferguson. Just before the expedition departed, one of Burke's fellow police officers warned him, 'You'll have to shoot that man yet.'

By any standards the expedition was a disparate group. Fletcher, Creber and Cowan had been sacked before the party left Royal Park, leaving five Irishmen, four 'Indians', three Englishmen, three Germans and an American. None had any real exploration experience. As the men began to size each other up, it became clear that the party was an uneasy fusion of personalities and motivations, unlikely to pull together in times of trouble. Burke's mission to reach the north coast first had become an obsession. Just before leaving Melbourne, he told his friend Charles Saint, 'I have only one ambition, which is to do some deed before I die, that shall entitle me to have my name honourably inscribed on the page of history. If I succeed in that I care not what death, or when I die.'

In contrast, his surveyor William Wills along with the artist

Ludwig Becker and the expedition doctor Hermann Beckler were expecting a genuine scientific examination of the continent. Landells cared little for either pursuit, as long as his own reputation remained intact, and it soon became clear he was volatile, stubborn and easily upset. Ferguson was a loose cannon and the remaining men were little more than enthusiastic amateurs.

And Burke had already deserted his officers. As his men struggled to set up their first camp in Essendon, the Irishman galloped back to Melbourne to see Julia Mathews perform one last time. His infatuation with Julia had only intensified. On 18 August 1860, he called together two of his confidants— Richard Nash, government storekeeper, and John Macadam, Royal Society's secretary—to have them witness his will. He left everything to Julia Mathews. It was a shocking gesture for an unmarried gentleman to leave all his worldly goods to an actress less than half his age.

After the performance Burke asked Julia to marry him, even offering to give up the expedition or postpone its departure if she would become his wife. Julia refused to give an immediate answer but after further persuasion she agreed to reconsider the offer once he returned. There was, at least, some hope. Newspapers noted that it wasn't until the next morning that the leader returned to camp. Robert O'Hara Burke set out the next day with a lock of Julia's hair in a pouch around his neck and reputedly with one of her tiny kid gloves in his pocket. His quest had begun.

FIVE

NO TEA, NO FIRE

AS Burke led his cavalcade through the towns and villages to the north of Melbourne, the 'Australian Sahara' must have seemed a million miles away. The rain was heavy and prolonged. Some days the hailstones were the size of billiard balls. At night, the men huddled around their campfires, smoking and sipping tea—but no matter how close they sat to the flames, their flannel trousers and woollen tops never really dried out. The canvas tents were saturated, and their sodden equipment was twice as heavy to lift.

Every day the roads deteriorated and the wheel ruts deepened. While the camels slithered through the bogs, the wagons ground to a halt. The expedition was in black soil country, where, in dry conditions, the dark earth bakes like concrete but rain transforms it into a natural skating rink. The back-breaking routine of keeping the wagons moving when their wheels were frequently disappearing into the quagmire resulted in an average speed of between one and five kilometres an hour.

The camels' progress was faster but equally precarious. The horny pads on their feet were designed for deserts, not swamps, and they slipped constantly. Fearing for their safety, Landells ordered that they were not to be ridden. On 22 August as the party headed for the village of Lancefield, sixty kilometres from Melbourne, Ludwig Becker trudged for ten hours through the mud. That evening he wrote in his diary: 'No tea, no fire; we slept in the wet.'

Becker had not expected to rip his hands to shreds leading camels and loading boxes each day. He was an officer, a biologist and a painter charged with recording the expedition's progress for posterity. He was also an early victim of the Royal Society's muddled objectives.

With its enormous procession of wagons and camels, the Victorian Exploring Expedition had all the appearances of a genuine scientific survey party and many Royal Society members still thought that a thorough investigation of the continent was about to take place. But others realised that Burke's appointment as leader had already destroyed any veneer of scientific credibility. If it hadn't been for the Royal Society's German contingent, Burke would have dispensed with the scientists altogether. But as a compromise he agreed to take Ludwig Becker to serve as 'artist and naturalist' and Hermann Beckler, a doctor and amateur botanist who could fulfil a dual role.

Hermann Beckler dreamed of a career as a biologist and botanist. For many years he tried to establish a medical practice to fund his passion but he struggled to earn a living, let alone undertake any journeys of his own. After a stint collecting specimens for Melbourne's botanical gardens, Beckler secured the backing of Mueller and applied to join the expedition.

The only member of the Royal Society to join Burke's party was Ludwig Becker—a charming eccentric who spent several years in the goldfields armed with a sketchpad and a pet bat. According to Lady Denison, the wife of Tasmania's lieutenant-governor:

He is a most amusing person, talks English badly but very energetically...he is rather shy and sensitive; but with all that he is very pleasing. He is one of those universal geniuses who do anything; is a very good naturalist; geologist etc., draws and plays and sings, conjures and ventriloquises and imitates the notes of birds so accurately that the wild birds will come to him at the sound of the call.

Burke was not impressed by Becker's character or his talent. He saw the fifty-two-year-old German as an encumbrance foisted on him by Mueller. After all, if a middle-aged scientist could cross the continent, Burke could hardly claim it was a colossal physical achievement.

The Royal Society's instructions to the scientists were as daunting as they were unrealistic. Hermann Beckler was expected to keep a diary of all the flora he observed, collect specimens in various stages of development, detail plants used by Aboriginal tribes as food and medicine, and undertake as many side-trips as possible to record the maximum number of new species. Ludwig Becker was to sketch the general terrain (with particular reference to watercourses and mineral formations) and collect and sketch specimens of all mammals, birds, fish and fossils found en route.

William Wills bore the heaviest burden. By day he was to keep detailed records: of distance travelled, general terrain, watercourses, water quality (including samples), geological formations, soil types (including samples), and occurrence of minerals or gems (including samples). He was to sketch specimens, draw updated maps daily, measure compass variations and record meteorological conditions, including rainfall, temperature, wind speeds, whirlwinds, thunderstorms, dust storms, mirages, refraction and magnetic observations. By night, Wills was expected to make astronomical observations including the 'paths of meteors' and the 'patterns of twinkling stars'.

Wills also had to navigate the party across the continent. He was, after all, the only member of the party fully conversant with taking star sightings and the only man practised in using a compass and sextant. Undeterred by this impossible workload, Wills soon devised a way of working as he rode:

> Riding on the camels is a much more pleasant process than I anticipated, and for my work I find it much better than riding on horseback. The saddles, as you are aware, are double, so I sit on the back portion behind the hump, and pack my instruments in front. I can thus ride on, keeping my journal and making calculations; and need only stop the camel when I want to take any bearings carefully; but the barometers can be read and registered without halting. The animals are very quiet, and easily managed, much more so than horses.

With the rain pelting down, no one was giving much thought to science. On the third day one of the sepoys, Samla, resigned. As a Hindu he was not allowed to eat the salt beef that was a staple of the explorers' diet. He had suffered in silence for two days on bread and water, before asking Landells if he could be discharged. He headed towards Melbourne, Ludwig Becker noted, 'his eyes full of tears'. Four of the original recruits had now left. Burke's response was to hire general labourers on a casual basis. Three men, Brooks, Lane and McIlwaine joined the party after it left Melbourne.

As the expedition inched north, the wagons broke down daily. Everyone who watched the expedition totter past reached the same conclusion: Burke's party had too many supplies and not enough transport. The expedition carried eight tonnes of food but this was not excessive considering it had to last nineteen men between eighteen months and two years. Although Burke had the final say, it was Ferdinand Mueller who drew up the original list of supplies, based on a formula devised by Augustus Gregory. He had discovered that the minimum daily ration required to keep his men healthy was: 500 grams of salt beef or pork, 500 grams of flour, twenty-one grams of coffee or seven grams of tea, eighty-five grams of sugar and a small measure of vinegar and lime juice to prevent scurvy. Mueller's list allowed for much the same nutritional intake but with more variety.

It was the other twelve tonnes that really slowed things down. The mounds of useless equipment were the result of an inexperienced commander with a free hand and an open chequebook. Were twelve sets of dandruff brushes and four enema kits really necessary? There were six tonnes of firewood, 200 kilograms of medications for the camels and horses and enough ammunition to win a small war. Luxuries were well catered for: a large bathtub, an oak and cedar table with two oak stools and forty-five yards of gossamer for fly veils. Yet the party took just two sets of field glasses, two watches and only twelve water bottles.

Before the expedition left, Burke turned the management of the stores over to Hermann Beckler, who was appalled at the purchase of so much equipment, 'on a scale out of all proportion to our means of transport'.

It had been intended to convey the bulk of the stores by ship via Adelaide and the Darling River as far as Menindee. Royal Society member and steamboat pioneer Captain Francis Cadell offered to provide the service free of charge. It would dispense with the need for wagons and save the horses and camels for the more arduous terrain further north.

But just forty-eight hours before the expedition was due to depart, Burke overturned the plan. He decided that transporting the supplies via Adelaide would give the South Australians an opportunity to interfere and delay proceedings. Also, Cadell had supported Warburton in the leadership battle and Burke didn't want to entrust the stores to an opponent. The alternative was to carry everything by wagon at vast expense. Beckler protested, yet Burke was adamant. He wanted full control and he was prepared to drag twenty tonnes of equipment along 750 kilometres of unmade roads to get it.

After the first few chaotic days a routine began to emerge. Each morning the men woke at dawn to the sound of a Chinese gong echoing through the gum trees. As smoke filled the air, tea was brewed and they breakfasted on hunks of damper filled with salt beef. If the horses and camels had been tethered or kept in paddocks the night before, little time was wasted catching them, but if they had been hobbled or let loose, it might require a walk of a few kilometres to recapture them before loading could begin.

It took between two and three hours to organise the packs, then hoist them onto the horses and camels using a pulley system slung over a tree branch. Often it was 9.30 before the main party set off, with Burke and the horses up ahead, followed by Landells and his camels, and the wagons grinding along behind.

The party travelled for up to twelve hours a day, exhausted by the time they reached camp but still with a couple of hours work ahead, feeding and watering the animals, unloading the supplies and mending broken equipment. By nightfall the tents were pitched, the campfire was crackling, the stew was bubbling and loaves of fresh damper sat swelling in the camp ovens. The officers retired to their tents to write up their journals and the men sat in the flickering light, smoking and telling yarns.

After a week, the expedition had only covered 100 kilometres and was camped at the hamlet of Mia Mia. Since it was a Sunday and the wagons were still bogged some kilometres behind, Burke allowed a rare day of rest.

For many small towns, the arrival of the expedition was the most exciting event in years. Settlers travelled from far and wide to see the people they had read so much about in the newspapers. One spectator reported:

> As we approached the Mia Mia hotel, we saw a long line of strange looking animals squatted alongside a fence…Occasional peculiar snorts emitted by the animals had a strange effect on our horses, and though we had ridden them so hard already, they seemed quite disposed to turn round and rush home again.

The next day, as the explorers set off towards Swan Hill, Hermann Beckler noticed for the first time that the countryside was changing:

> There is nothing more interesting than this sharp frontier between the coastal land and the inland, continental regions… one now finds oneself in the inland, and however far one penetrates into the heart of the continent, the landscape of the coastal fringe is left behind forever.

The small farms gave way to the more ancient panorama of the Terrick Terrick Plains. Becker was now in open country:

The effect when one sees extensive plains for the first time is somewhat very peculiar: the plain looks like a calm ocean with green water…On you go, miles and miles, a single tree, a belt of timber appeared at the horizon affected by the mirage; you reach that belt of small trees, a Wallaby, a kangerooh-rat disturbs for a moment the monotony, and a few steps further on you are again on the green calm ocean.

The expedition may have looked impressive as it marched across the plains, but tensions were already apparent. Burke had little patience with either the camels or the scientists but provided they maintained a reasonable pace he was happy to ignore them as far as possible. He rode on ahead, leaving Landells, Wills, Beckler and Becker to travel on foot dragging their animals through the mud. Morale sagged and resentment germinated. Burke aggravated the situation by retiring to the nearest pub or farmhouse in the evenings, instead of camping near his men.

Landells was worried that Burke was in too much of a hurry. The camels had little time to graze and even at this early stage the heavy conditions were taking their toll. Beckler confirmed his fears. 'Within five days the camels began to show the effects of continual rain, the gradual change of feed and camping in the open. They developed catarrhs and diarrhoea and their faeces contained their hitherto customary feed, gram [an Indian fodder], in an undigested state.'

The problem was that Burke had so much to prove. The Melbourne newspapers had jeered at his lack of experience and as the expedition passed near Bendigo, the *Advertiser* increased his sense of insecurity by singling out Landells as the real leader.

So far the reception from settlers along the way had been friendly, even though the camels scattered livestock and the wagons destroyed the flooded roads. Word had spread that Burke was in a hurry with 'money to burn' so the locals charged outrageously for fodder and accommodation en route. Costs began to escalate as goods became more expensive to the north of Bendigo. The settlements thinned out to a scattering of shepherds' huts and a few Aboriginal camps. Hermann Beckler climbed a small hill to take in the surreal beauty of the natural landscape:

> The play of sunlight and clouds produced wonderful effects on the wide plain; light and shadow alternated in quick succession as in a diorama. Miles of land were lit up, only to be cast into deepest shadow within a few seconds. Huge clouds sailed across the sky and their shadows rolled over the land like the tatters of a gigantic, torn veil.

The weather deteriorated again and Burke was forced to schedule another rest day after the entire expedition became saturated on a thirty-four-kilometre trek towards Mount Hope. The wagons got stuck and, on his way back to retrieve them, Charles Ferguson got lost, fell into a pit and knocked himself unconscious. It was several hours before he came to and managed to rejoin the expedition.

On 6 September, the party reached Swan Hill on the Murray River, 320 kilometres from Melbourne. Here Burke intended to rest for a couple of days and prepare for the next leg of the journey towards Menindee, but when he arrived an urgent telegram was waiting for him: a warrant was being sought for his arrest.

SIX

FIFTY-SIX DAYS

THE telegram threatened Burke with imprisonment for a dishonoured personal cheque for £96. It was a serious matter. It could endanger Burke's standing with the Royal Society and particularly with Sir William Stawell. In panic, he wrote to his friend Richard Nash, asking him to stand security for his debt (which he did), but since his letters would take several days to reach Melbourne he had no way of knowing if the matter had been resolved.

Swan Hill (named by Thomas Mitchell in a temper after the birds that kept him awake at night) was not a happy town for explorers. Burke fretted about the cheque and worried that gossip about the expedition would find its way back to Melbourne. The wagons were still three days adrift and their drivers were demanding more pay by the hour. Charles Ferguson remarked later:

> He was kind and generous to a fault but let anything happen out of the routine he was confused, then excited until finally he would lose all control of his better judgement. Then again when he had made up his mind to do something he never considered the consequences. He had thorough discipline and no one dared to presume to contradict him.

The arrival of the Royal Society's Georg Neumayer only increased Burke's paranoia. The professor joined the explorers in Swan Hill as part of his survey of the earth's magnetism. He intended to travel with the party towards Menindee, a small settlement by the Darling River.

Nearly three weeks into the journey, Burke realised that his party was crippled by the weight of its supplies. The committee was insisting that he get rid of the wagons as soon as possible but, having refused Cadell's offer of river transport, how else was he to carry all his supplies to the proposed depot at Cooper Creek?

Having placed himself in an impossible situation, Burke called his officers together to secure their support, then wrote to the committee justifying their 'joint decision' to retain the wagons as far as Menindee:

> I am well aware that our baggage is cumbersome and that a time will I hope soon come when we shall be obliged to have the greater part of it behind us, but to do so now, before having established our Depot upon the Darling, where every article may be of the greatest service, would I think be a most danger-ous injudicious proceeding.

The idea of a depot on the Darling River was new. Burke was deviating from his instructions to form the expedition's base camp at Cooper Creek. So was the Darling camp an addition to the original plan or a replacement for it? Burke most likely realised that it would be hard enough to drag his entire outfit as far as Menindee. After that, he would have to improvise.

Swan Hill seemed reluctant to relinquish the explorers to the desert—on 12 September there was a rowdy farewell as the party was bombarded with old boots and handfuls of rice for good luck. One observer noticed that Burke wiped his eyes and seemed 'visibly affected by the genuine kindness he had met with'.

The party that crossed the Murray was very different from

the one that had rolled out of Melbourne. Only fourteen of the original nineteen members remained. At Swan Hill, Burke discharged the sepoy Esau Khan, who had become too ill to work. He also let go Brooks, Lane and John Polongeaux, a Frenchman, whom he had hired near Bendigo a few days earlier. Four new men joined the expedition. Alexander MacPherson was a blacksmith and saddler, William Hodgkinson a journalist, and Charley Gray an ex-sailor. Robert Bowman had previously accompanied both Augustus and Charles Gregory on expeditions in northern and central Australia. Aside from the Gregory brothers he was probably the most experienced explorer in Australia and a valuable addition to Burke's outfit.

With so many people coming and going, it was difficult to establish any sense of unity. In particular, the men disliked their high-handed American foreman Charles Ferguson. When Ferguson began to complain about his pay, Burke retaliated by attempting to reduce his salary even further. A row ensued in which the foreman threatened to resign. Burke backed down. Ferguson stayed on.

It took the remodelled party three days to reach the hamlet of Balranald in New South Wales. The journey had been dogged by bad weather yet again and the roads were now so bad that the wagon drivers insisted their loads be reduced or their horses would collapse. The result was an impromptu public auction. After hauling his supplies for more than 400 kilometres, Burke sold off equipment in the middle of nowhere. Some things (two full sets of blacksmiths' tools, assorted firearms, the camel stretcher) had always been superfluous but many explorers would have regarded other items as essential, in particular, supplies of lime juice to prevent scurvy.

To cut costs further, Burke decided to discharge six more men at Balranald, yet he had trouble confronting anyone with the news. Instead of paying the men and letting them go, Burke told Becker, Ferguson, Brahe, Langan, McIlwaine and Belooch to stay behind at Balranald, assuring them he would send for them later on.

For several hours the camp was on the brink of mutiny. Ferguson challenged his leader to a fight and had to be restrained. At first, Burke insisted that he wanted the American to stay, but later he called Ferguson aside and told him, 'You surmised right; it was just as you thought. I intended to leave you before but I could not tell you of it.' Burke then offered to retain Ferguson and Langan at reduced salaries. When they refused, he issued their wage cheques—but since shopkeepers and bank-tellers knew that the expedition was in financial trouble, no one was willing to cash them.

Burke must have changed his mind again because a few hours later Becker, Brahe and Belooch rejoined the main party. He was, however, determined to rid himself of Ferguson, Langan and McIlwaine, who chased the party for thirty-five kilometres to beg for enough money to return to Melbourne. Finally the trio turned south, threatening to sue Burke for wrongful dismissal.

This debacle did nothing to improve Burke's reputation. In Balranald, the general opinion was that he was 'thoroughly deficient in experience'. Settlers noticed that 'Camping places were not selected until after dark, sometimes till after midnight, when it could not be seen whether there might be any food for the cattle [camels] or not. At every camp, lots of tools, axes and spades were left.' As the expedition left for Menindee, Burke travelled ahead with the expedition party and camels and left the wagons to follow under Beckler's supervision.

Against local advice, Burke decided that instead of following the recognised track from Balranald to the Darling River, he would cut across country. Beckler was exasperated. 'Why did we have to experiment just here? It was the "shortest route", the straight line that once again led Mr Burke into temptation.' Burke's route took his party across 'mallee country'—'no one knows who invented the mallee,' locals commented 'but the devil is strongly suspected'.

The sandhill terrain was a 'wild wasteland', 'hell on earth' for the wagon drivers. While Burke rode on ahead with Wills, the wagons crawled through the heavy sand at just one or two kilometres an hour. By 25 September, just over a week after leaving Balranald, the draught horses were too exhausted to go any further. They were unhitched and driven on to a waterhole, leaving the wagons abandoned in the scrub. Burke's 'short cut' meant that the forward party had to traverse the mallee country three times to rescue the wagons.

Georg Neumayer finished collecting his 'magnetic data' and was anxious to return to Melbourne. Since the professor had ridden on ahead for much of the time, he avoided the fiasco of the wagons and formed a positive impression of the expedition. In fact Burke, Wills and Neumayer had become increasingly friendly as they rode together. On 28 September, as Neumayer was packing up, the three men sat up into the night, discussing the possibility of sending a relief vessel to the north coast to meet the expedition. It was agreed that Burke would write to the committee from Menindee if such a ship were necessary.

As soon as Neumayer disappeared over the horizon Burke started to dismantle any remaining vestige of scientific credibility surrounding the expedition. Free at last to do as he pleased without reports being taken back to the Royal Society, Burke confronted the scientists. It was the mild-mannered Becker who bore the brunt of his dissatisfaction:

> Before we marched Mr Burke told us that, from today, we had to walk inch for inch, all the way up to the Gulf of Carpentaria, as all the camels and horses were required to carry stores etc. To Dr Beckler and me he said: 'now Gentleman from this time you have to give up your scientific investigations but to work like the rest of the men…'

Burke told all his men that henceforth they would be allowed just fifteen kilograms of personal equipment each. For the scientists, this meant leaving behind nearly all their instruments—from now on they were little more than glorified camel hands.

Then, Burke turned on Landells. He insisted that in order to lighten the wagons, each camel would have to carry an extra 180 kilograms. With heavy rain and thunderstorms drenching the campsite, the stores were reorganised yet again. The new regime brought nothing but misery for Becker:

> Having had no sleep for the last two nights but plenty of hard work during the day-time I felt somewhat unwell, however I began work as usual at 5 o'clock in the morning. We commenced saddling and loading the camels and were ready to start by 11 o'clock…None of us was told how far or how long we had this day, or rather the rest of this day, to travel, and as nothing but tea and biscuit with a little cold mutton was served out early in the morning, and we had no food before starting, I thought, in a few hours we would halt on some waterhole to take there the required nourishment—but…we marched on without rest and food for twenty-four miles over high hills covered with a deep, loose sand, and arrived at night at a plain containing some

water. I had no food for nearly three days; partly in consequence of my own indisposition, and no sleep for two nights, and had to pull, in the heat of the day, three camels for 24 miles through the most wretched country—it was quite natural I should feel weak. It was about sunset when I asked Mr Landells to stop only 5 minutes so as to be able to recover myself as I felt like fainting.

Becker's suffering was no accident. In a letter to his friend Frederick Standish, Burke revealed:

You should have seen old B——'s face upon my announcing that all the officers would have to act as working men, and that we shall only carry 30 lb weight of baggage for each man. Loading four camels and then marching 20 miles is no joke. The first two days of it nearly cooked poor B——, and I think he will not be able to stand it much longer.

Burke ordered Landells not to let Becker ride at all, but to 'walk him until he gave in'. Ludwig Becker refused to give up and still managed to complete seven beautiful sketches on his way to the Darling. He had become the unwitting object of a power struggle between Burke and Landells. As the expedition approached the Darling River, it threatened to blow the party apart.

George Landells was incensed that the camels were fully loaded before the expedition had even reached the edge of the desert. And Burke's hostility towards the camels led to a shift in alliances. Landells was left to his own devices and at the same time, both Becker and Beckler begin to mention that 'Mr Wills was left in charge' of certain matters. Burke was sidelining his deputy and confiding more and more in his surveyor.

Late on 2 October the expedition reached Bilbarka on the Darling River. Here Burke learned that a steamer, the *Moolge-wanke*, was heading north to Menindee. Seizing the opportunity to rid himself of the wagons, Burke ordered his men to prepare eight tonnes of equipment to be loaded onto the steamer. While this was being done, Burke bickered with his deputy, sending ripples of tension through the camp. Their latest disagreement was about the 270 litres of rum that Landells had insisted on bringing as medicine for the camels. Burke demanded that the rum be left behind, accused Landells of pampering the camels, slowing down the expedition and offering the wrong advice. Landells stormed off, saying Burke was a madman who would get them all killed:

> His conduct throughout has displayed such want of judgement, candour, and decision, as at once to destroy my entire confidence and respect. Indeed, that conduct has been altogether of such an extraordinary character, that I have on several occasions grave doubts about his sanity. His temper was quite ungovernable. He usually carried loaded firearms, and I often was fearful that he would use them dangerously while in a passion.

Accounts differ on how the quarrel was resolved but, whatever the details, the result was melodramatic and undignified. According to Landells, Burke burst into tears and begged his deputy to stay, saying, 'My God! I never thought you would leave me, as I have great dependence in you. Come on: I hope none of the men have seen this.' According to Burke, Landells wanted to return to Melbourne, claiming he had only ever agreed to go as far as the Darling. According to Wills, Landells maintained he had a 'secret agreement' with the committee and would continue only if he had complete control over the camels. When Burke threatened to withhold his pay for 'disgraceful behaviour', Landells backed down and agreed to stay on.

Wills' prominent role in the proceedings revealed his growing influence on the management of the expedition. The surveyor respected Landells' work with the camels but nevertheless decided he was 'nothing of gentleman, either in manners or feeling'.

While the camp seethed with gossip, the camels vanished into the bush. Hodgkinson, King, McDonough and Dost Mohomet set out to find them, but got lost themselves. Landells and Belooch then couldn't find either the men or the camels, forcing Burke and Becker to light fires and sound the Chinese gong to guide everyone home. King, McDonough, Dost Mohomet, Landells and Belooch returned that night but Hodgkinson did not come back until noon the next day. No one found the camels.

Burke was so enraged that he considered abandoning the camels altogether. It was only when Burke paid an Aboriginal tracker £5 that the camels were located. 'Them long-neck yarrowman' were grazing just a kilometre away from the camp.

The rum was left behind along with boxes of stores. When the party finally departed for Menindee on 11 October, the atmosphere was tense. Determined to prove he could keep pace with Burke's horses, Landells drove the camels long into the night and Becker was once again caught in the crossfire:

> We had no food and no water, and the moon was down—but a few matches assisted us in looking for the track. On we went for miles and miles; Mr Landells, staggering in front, was scarcely able to keep himself free from falling asleep; I,

behind, pulling the camels and looking out anxiously for our camp-fire…

Three days later, Becker's horse trod on his foot, leaving the artist barely able to walk. Burke was forced to allow him to ride one of the horses.

By pushing his animals to the limit, Landells arrived in Menindee on 15 October just twenty-four hours after Burke. Leaving his exhausted animals under the shade of the river red gums on the banks of the Darling, the camel driver went triumphantly to report his arrival. But it was not Burke who awaited him in the leader's tent. It was Wills, and he calmly told Landells that he was fired.

Landells accused Burke of insanity. The Irishman responded by branding his deputy a scoundrel and challenged him to a duel with pistols. Landells refused, saying he had come to 'fight the desert', not his commanding officer.

The next morning, as if to prove he could dispense with Landells' expertise, Burke had the camels lined up and fitted with special ropes attached to their nose-pegs. The animals bellowed as they were led towards the slippery riverbank. To Landells' consternation, the camels were about to be swum across the Darling in defiance of his recommendation that they be ferried by boat.

Burke deliberately placed Wills in command of the operation, declaring that if such a 'trifling obstacle' as the Darling River was enough to stop the animals, then they 'would be of little use upon the contemplated journey'. As Landells stood glowering on the sidelines, each camel swam across the muddy waters. His humiliation was complete. He packed his bags and arranged to travel back to Melbourne. Wills informed the rest of the party of Landells' resignation. By nightfall Wills' position was official—Burke had promoted him to the post of deputy leader.

Later that evening, Beckler too announced his resignation. 'It was no little matter for me,' he admitted, 'to draw back from a wish nurtured so ardently and for so long as this expedition.'

Rumours swirled down the Darling and resurfaced in newspaper editorials nearer Melbourne:

> The opinion of parties able to judge on the Darling is that Mr Burke will not be able to make any more than 200 miles beyond the settled districts this season, and that he is not the right man for the work he has undertaken. It is stated that instead of making himself agreeable to the men, he harasses them soldier style and in going to camp at night will not allow a man to dismount until he gives the word, although he may be a mile away.

The Victorian Exploring Expedition had disintegrated on the easiest section of the journey and was now lying in tatters on the edge of the desert. The journey of 750 kilometres from Melbourne to Menindee had taken fifty-six days—a horseman could ride it in ten. Of the nineteen original recruits, eleven had resigned or been dismissed. Eight more men had been hired. Five of these had also left.

The most significant departure, aside from Landells, was that of Robert Bowman. Beckler noted that Bowman 'did not like it with us at all and left us after only a few days'. Another account says that Bowman contrasted 'the superior skill of Gregory with the bungling of the Victorian leader'.

Now, perched on the outskirts of European civilisation, Burke faced the challenge of rescuing the expedition before it disappeared behind the 'shimmering veils' of the desert. The next stage of the journey would take Burke to the very edge of the map—Cooper Creek. From now on there would be no tracks, no signposts and no local information, save for the wisdom of the indigenous people who lived along the route.

SEVEN

SPLITTING THE PARTY

MENINDEE was as far as European settlement had penetrated. It lay in Baagandji Aboriginal territory and took its name inexplicably from their term *milhthaka*, meaning egg yolk. There were a few bark huts, a pub, a store and a police station. Only the Darling River brought the area to life.

Menindee owed its continued survival to the riverboat pioneer Francis Cadell. He set up a fortnightly steamer service and a small trading post in 1859. When the river was high enough, boats brought supplies up from Adelaide and returned south with cargoes of wool. Once the shearing was finished, the only entertainment was to drink rum until the heat, the flies and the dust melted into oblivion.

The expedition had reached Menindee far later than expected. It was the 'wrong time of year' to leave the safety of the Darling River system for Cooper Creek, nearly 600 kilometres to the north. Summer was beginning to shrivel the waterholes, but Burke was determined to push on. Before resigning, Landells and Beckler had petitioned strongly to wait out the summer on the banks of the Darling. They argued that since the expedition had missed the cool season, it would be better to stay where there was access to fresh supplies. But the thought of delaying for another three months only seemed to exacerbate Burke's desire to escape.

Transport (too little) and supplies (too many) were still the expedition's main problems. To make matters worse, as the men unloaded the rations from the *Moolgewanke*, they discovered the dried 'pemmican' meat had rotted. If the whole party was to reach the Cooper, it would take at least a month to procure fresh supplies of dried meat.

Perhaps the answer lay in reducing the party? Burke's instructions, however, required him to take his entire outfit to Cooper Creek. The alternative was to send a forward party up to the Cooper with half the supplies, then return the pack animals to retrieve the remainder. This was a risky option. Burke had few experienced men, insufficient animals and only one qualified navigator.

Burke's solution was to extract the 'best' elements of his party for himself and leave the remainder behind to fend for themselves. He decided to take Wills, John King (to look after the camels), William Brahe, William Patten, Thomas McDonough, Charley Gray and Dost Mohomet, along with three-quarters of his remaining horses and camels. This would leave the rest of the men plus seven horses and ten camels on the banks of the Darling with a vague promise that they would be called up to the Cooper later.

On 17 October, in a final hollow gesture towards scientific endeavour, Burke invited Becker to join the forward party, saying:

> If you like to be with the party, you are welcome, but I must tell you, there is no time for scientific researches, nor a horse or camel to ride on, you will have to tramp all the way, and must do the work like the other men.

Burke knew Becker had injured his foot and would have no choice but to refuse. Having discarded the expedition's 'dead wood', Burke retired to the Menindee pub, where he fell into conversation with a local man named William Wright.

Wright was a man of few words, a hardened bushman with weatherbeaten hands and a slow direct manner. He had just returned from a 250-kilometre journey towards Cooper Creek and was keen to explore further. Several drinks later, Wright volunteered as a guide and Burke accepted. Wright suggested leaving Menindee as soon as possible. He also recommended keeping the expedition together so the entire outfit could reach the Cooper while the waterholes were full.

Burke took the first piece of advice and ignored the second. He asked Hermann Beckler to take charge of a rearguard camp with just four men: Becker, MacPherson, Belooch and Hodgkinson. Beckler was unenthusiastic but agreed to stay on until a replacement officer could be found.

Burke told Ludwig Becker, 'I intend to look for a road up to Coopers Creek, and how the way is, and about the water; and as soon as I have found a spot where to form a depot, I shall send for you to come up with the others and with such things as wanted.' But did he really mean to fetch up the rearguard party and make a depot on the Cooper or was he just setting up a quick dash for the north coast? Burke's intentions are difficult to decipher. He kept no written records and issued no written instructions to his subordinates.

If Burke was genuinely planning to reunite his party, he never made it clear whether he expected the remaining men to make their own way to the Cooper with the animals they had left, or whether he would send back extra transport to help them. Either way, his strategy made little sense. From now on, valuable supplies

THE GREAT AUSTRALIAN EXPLORATION RACE.

This Melbourne *Punch* cartoon was drawn by Nicholas Chevalier at the height of the inter-colonial rivalry between Victoria and South Australia. The public loved the idea of a race between Burke and Stuart.

would be in Menindee, while the men who needed them most were out in the desert.

Perhaps the biggest reason for Burke's decision to leave so soon had arrived aboard the *Moolgewanke*. It carried South Australian newspapers revealing that John McDouall Stuart had failed in his attempt to cross the continent. He had just returned to Adelaide after a journey that had taken him to within 800 kilometres of the north coast. He had planted a Union Jack in the centre of Australia, and then continued north, only to be turned back on 26 June 1860 by an Aboriginal ambush near the present-day town of Tennant Creek.

Burke guessed that it would not be long before his rival set out again. In the meantime he had at least a two-month head start and he was determined not to squander it. Stuart's failure had given him a real chance of success.

On 19 October 1860, a new incarnation of the Victorian Exploring Expedition left Menindee. There were eight Europeans, two Aboriginal guides and a string of sixteen camels and nineteen horses. Burke must have felt an overwhelming sense of relief— the wagons and the scientists were gone, he had escaped any censure from the committee, and he was at least two months ahead of John McDouall Stuart. At last the politics were over and the journey into the unknown had begun. Undaunted by the 600 kilometres of wilderness that lay between him and Cooper Creek, Burke wrote to the committee just before he left Menindee: 'I still feel as confident as ever in the success of the main object of the Expedition.'

Just what was the 'main object' of the expedition? All pretence of scientific research had been abandoned. Somehow, between Melbourne and Menindee, the expedition had metamorphosed into a unit strikingly similar to Stuart's lightweight outfit. Was such a transformation inevitable, or was it a deliberate policy to whittle down the group once it was beyond the public gaze? If so—was it Burke's idea alone or was there a secret official plan?

There is now evidence to show that there had always been a secret plot to divide the expedition. Early in 1860, a small group of men recognised its potential role in opening up northern Australia for commercial exploitation. Among them was Sir William Stawell and other committee members such as Thomas Embling,

Richard Eades and John Macadam. They wanted to develop an overland route to a northern port. Aside from the telegraph, it would also allow a direct commercial link to south-east Asia.

It had also come to light that a large area of land between the 141st and 138th meridians had not been included in the colony when it was first proclaimed. Technically the land belonged to New South Wales. But New South Wales wasn't interested in the land, and it was waiting for the first group who established a route to the Gulf of Carpentaria on Australia's north coast. This may have accounted for the sudden change to the expedition's instructions in June 1860, from a north-western route towards to the Victoria River to a more direct journey north towards the Gulf.

Embling and Stawell pondered the possibilities and developed an ambitious scheme. They enlisted the tacit support of several other politicians including the chief secretary John O'Shanassy for the expedition to explore more than just the flora and fauna of northern Australia. Victoria was rich but small. Perhaps its future lay in the annexation of a northern territory? An expedition cloaked in scientific respectability might also make a secret push for the Gulf and secure the prize before another colony got a chance.

It has always been assumed that it was Burke's decision to split his party at Menindee, but certain members of the Exploration Committee had never intended the whole party to cross the continent. In a letter, written the day before the expedition left Melbourne, from prominent Royal Society member Alfred Selwyn to his friend Harry, Selwyn admits the party will divide at Cooper Creek.

My dear Harry,

Would you like to join the Exploring Party? Another surveyor is wanted and I think you would be just the man if your wishes are that way inclined. The pay would be less than you make now and you would of course have to go second to Wills, who is already appointed and be under him while you were together, but that would probably not be for long—*as the party will have to divide after leaving Cooper's Creek and a surveyor be attached to each.* [italics added]

The secret plan to divide the party and allow Burke to 'make a dash for it' is reinforced by a letter to the expedition leader from Georg Neumayer in Melbourne, written on 25 October 1860 a few days after Burke had left Menindee. Burke and Neumayer had been discussing the necessity for a second surveyor but Neumayer admitted the plan was proving impossible to implement, 'I tried in vain to get another surveyor sent after you…There is underground work going on—I am sure about it. I have done my duty. You may be sure about it.' The professor wrote that he had also tried to arrange a ship to meet Burke when he reached the north coast so far without success. But Neumayer's letter never reached Burke. This meant Burke set out knowing that he couldn't rely on a rescue vessel and would therefore have to cross the continent in both directions. He also departed under the misguided impression that Neumayer could procure a second surveyor to join the rearguard party in Menindee.

In Melbourne George Landells' resignation was causing a major scandal. The camel driver had rushed back to the city to tell his side of the story, but in the end Burke won the public relations battle by two newspapers to one. The *Age* was his major supporter. It decided that the Irishman had shown 'firmness and self-reliance' by reducing his party, that Landells should have 'resigned in peace and with dignified self-respect, without seeking to make himself appear an ill-used man, and Mr Burke a crack-brained tyrant'.

The *Argus* agreed but the *Herald* decided it was Burke's fault: 'he had already demonstrated his total incapacity to hold his party firmly in hand, and that of itself is a very grave deduction from his concrete merits as a leader'.

As more revelations emerged, the members of the Royal Society squirmed with embarrassment. On his return to Melbourne, Neumayer attempted to subdue the scandal by holding a public meeting to defend the expedition. He emphasised Burke's 'wisdom' and 'judicious' behaviour. 'There was not one man who was not pleased with the excellent leader placed over him,' he declared. The only concession to reality was an acknowledgment that 'Mr Burke might require some assistance in some scientific matters connected with the journey'.

The committee was by now facing financial problems. An audit revealed that £4500 had been spent to equip the party, one-third more than expected. The hired wagons added another £700, which left only enough to pay the men's salaries until the end of the year. By late October, even the tiny store in Menindee was refusing credit for the back-up party. Beckler and Becker had to search their packs for loose change every time they needed so much as a stamp or a new bootlace. The Royal Society was forced to approach the government for more funds and the chief secretary William Nicholson had little choice but to grant another £6000.

Meanwhile Burke was making excellent progress towards Cooper Creek. It was a more harmonious group that trekked north hour after hour. Wright and his Aboriginal trackers proved to be able guides and water was readily available. The environment was like nothing the men had ever seen before. 'This last season,' Wills wrote, 'is said to have been the most rainy that they have had for several years; yet everything looked so parched up that I should have imagined it had been an exceedingly dry one.'

North of the Darling, Aboriginal tribes such as the Danggali, the Wiljali, the Bandjgali, the Karennggapa and the Kullila all moved around according to the seasons, the locations of the game and the state of the waterholes. These survival skills had been perfected over many thousands of years. Burke made no attempt to learn these patterns of coexistence with the landscape. He marched for up to sixteen hours a day, often passing excellent water in the afternoon and camping late at night. There were no rest days. For now, the favourable conditions allowed him to get away with it but his rapid progress also gave him a false sense of security.

One hundred and twenty-five kilometres north of Menindee, the expedition passed through the Bynguano Ranges, a striking mountainous plateau that rises high above kilometres of flat waterless plains. Known as Mutawintji or Mootwingee, the area remains sacred for the Wilyakali tribe and many other Aboriginal groups.

Mutawintji is a haunting spiritual world. The plants, the trees, the earth, even the smell is different. Deep inside the network of red gorges, the narrow tumbling gullies hide dark silent pools, surrounded by some of the most sacred Aboriginal art.

Mutawintji had been a place of ceremony and celebration for indigenous people for thousands of years before Burke and

Wills arrived. With its permanent supply of water and game, it also provided a sort of emergency larder, a place of refuge that was not permanently occupied by any particular tribe so its resources were never squandered.

The explorers arrived with a different perspective. They spent just a few hours in one of the state's richest geological, biological, botanical and anthropological areas. Too busy to appreciate the subtleties before them, they filled their waterbags and left, describing the area as 'dark and gloomy'.

Burke was consumed by his desire to beat Stuart. William Brahe recalled later that speed dominated the expedition's daily routine:

> Delay of any kind chafed Burke. The only angry word I ever had from him was in consequence of it. Some packs had shifted; the horses were delayed. He rode back, asking impatiently what was wrong. I explained, and said 'It's all right.' 'It's not all right,' he exclaimed angrily. 'It's all wrong!' and rode away. In two hours he was back, saying kindly, 'You must be very tired Brahe. Ride my horse for a while.' He would blaze up into a temper very quickly, but soon got over it.

The rest of the men had no choice but to keep up. Wills continued with his special 'camel-back' system to record information. He amazed everyone with his stamina. Long after the others had crawled inside their bedrolls, he stayed up to take his nightly observations and plot the party's position.

Burke did not keep a diary at all along this stretch of the journey, relying on his deputy to record any geographical features. Wills was surprised at the variety of the landscape. It alternated between 'as good grazing country as one would wish to see' and dusty clay flats so barren 'one might almost fancy himself in another planet'.

Ten days after leaving Menindee, on 29 October, the explorers reached a low-lying fertile area known as the Torowoto Swamp, 250 kilometres north of Menindee. With the journey progressing so well, Burke was increasingly impressed with William Wright's abilities as a bushman. At Torowoto, he made Wright his third-in-command and the next morning announced his intention to proceed to the Cooper at once. Wright was to return to Menindee with the Aboriginal trackers and retrieve the remainder of the stores. Burke outlined his plan, then offered each man the chance to turn back if they wished. All refused.

As usual Burke did not issue written instructions. In this case they would have been superfluous since Wright was nearly illiterate. Nevertheless, he did send a dispatch to the committee:

> Mr Wright returns from here to Menindie. I informed him that I should consider him third officer of the expedition, subject to the approval of the committee, from the day of our departure from Menindie, and I hope that they will confirm the appointment. In the mean time I have instructed him to follow me up with the remainder of the camels to Cooper's Creek, to take steps to procure a supply of jerked meat…I shall proceed on from here to Cooper's Creek. I may, or may not, be able to send back from there until we are followed up. Perhaps it would not be prudent to divide the party; the natives here have told Mr Wright that we shall meet with opposition on our way there. Perhaps I might find it advisable to leave a depot at Cooper's Creek, and go on with a small party to examine the country beyond it.
>
> Under any circumstance it is desirable that we should be followed up.

The letter was alarmingly imprecise and ominous in its use of the word 'perhaps'. It didn't clarify whether Wright was to wait until his appointment was confirmed before bringing up the stores or whether he would be receiving extra pack animals for transport. Burke's accompanying letter to his uncle only increased the confusion:

> I shall proceed on from here to Cooper's Creek or the Victoria River as it is sometimes called, and from thence to Carpentaria as straight as I can go and *if* I can go…It is very possible that I may leave half the party behind and push on with the rest if I find I cannot get through with them all.

With the promise that a second surveyor would be sent from Melbourne, Burke might have been justified in assuming that his rearguard party would at least be able to navigate to the Cooper. But he seemed to have forgotten that he had left just a handful of exhausted camels and horses in Menindee to haul tonnes of supplies 600 kilometres through the desert.

As Wright dissolved away into the horizon, so did the expedition's last link with civilisation. A man who had been running a sheep station two weeks earlier was now Burke's only lifeline.

EIGHT

─────────

COOPER'S CREEK

THE eight men toiled towards the Cooper with their camels slapping across the claypans and crunching over the rock-strewn plains. Their task was relentless, but they were lucky enough to be travelling in a benign season and, contrary to most desert treks, they were short of water for just one day on their entire journey. After twenty-three days, on 11 November 1860, they entered an undulating area of stony rises, little realising that the desert was about to perform one of its most startling transformations. The clues were subtle—a faint green sheen on the horizon, the rustle of a lizard in the scrub, a flock of birds in the distance.

The rich green environment that suddenly confronted the party was a revelation. Ahead was Cooper Creek, winding its way through the wilderness like a fat orange snake. The tired and dusty convoy of men, horses and camels plunged down its banks, and threw themselves into the water. The men were exultant; they were almost halfway across the continent and in terms of European exploration they were nearing the edge of the map.

Burke and Wills had reached one of the world's most remote river systems. Most of the time the Cooper is a series of transient waterholes fed by a network of streams. Defying convention, the water flows away from the coast through thousands of small arterial channels. In an 'average season', the giant Cooper system might flow for just a few hours or a few days, but in an exceptional year torrents of water spill out into lakes up to 100 kilometres wide. Perhaps just once or twice in a century, the deluge rushes south with such momentum that it sweeps across more than a thousand kilometres of arid land to fill Lake Eyre—one of the world's largest salt lakes. Briefly, the mythical inland sea that fascinated Charles Sturt becomes a reality.

One season might yield a beautiful chain of waterholes, bristling with life; the next will leave a series of mud-holes harbouring the skeletons of those unable to find sanctuary elsewhere.

Writing about the area in the 1930s, journalist Ernestine Hill gave this haunting insight into the cruelty of the landscape:

> Three hundred cattle were grouped about the borehead, in horribly lifelike attitudes, except that the eye sockets were empty. They had been dead for three years. Many had died standing and sitting, and sunk down only a little deeper in the sand. Hides and horns were mummified in that dry air. They were denied the mercy of decay.

When the expedition arrived at the beginning of the summer in 1860, they found it lush with green foliage, river red gums and coolibahs. They did not realise how lucky they were.

After the emptiness of the desert plains, the Cooper was brimming with life. While pelicans and spoonbills patrolled the creek, turtles and water rats foraged along the banks. There were echidnas, goannas, water dragons and birds. Some of the world's deadliest snakes slid through the undergrowth: the king brown, the death adder, and the fierce snake, whose fangs could inject enough venom to kill a hundred men.

Even the nights were noisy, as marsupial mice, possums and

bilbies looked for insects, and the air became choked with the calls of cicadas, crickets and frogs.

For the local Aboriginal tribes, the recent rains had produced a feast along the creek. Despite the unpredictability of their environment, indigenous people had lived and thrived around the Cooper or Kini-papa for more than 20,000 years. There were four main groups in the area, each comprised of about five hundred people: the Ngurawola, the Wangkamurra, the Yawarrawarrka and the Yandruwandha. The last two groups were closely related and it was their land that Burke and Wills were exploring as they moved up the creek.

They were a tall, athletic people, who used nothing more than a string girdle or a smearing of goanna fat to protect themselves from the elements. Many decorated themselves with necklaces and bangles made from brightly coloured seeds, shells and even human teeth. The men dressed their hair with feathers and knotted their beards into a distinctive loop tied with fur string. All the tribes were nomadic hunter-gatherers, moving around in small groups as their water and food supplies allowed. Possessions were limited, perhaps just a fire-making stick, a dish and a digging implement.

They lived in temporary shelters made of branches, known by the Europeans as wurleys, gunyahs or mia-mias. When the seasons were favourable, the people built villages near waterholes, constructing beehive-shaped huts, which were thatched and then covered in earth.

As the Cooper provided permanent water, it was the hub of a busy trade route through Aboriginal Australia that stretched as far afield as the Flinders Ranges in South Australia and Boulia in Queensland.

The locals were experts at finding water, digging in the right spots in the dried-up creek beds or tracking animals and birds to rock pools and soaks. They could also get water from certain roots and plant stems, even a particular type of frog, which was dug up and squeezed until its bloated body yielded a stream of precious liquid.

For Aboriginal people life is inextricably bound to the land, its features, rhythms, animals and its spirits. After researching the tribes around the Cooper for many years, historian Helen Tolcher concluded that:

> Time had no past, present or future, but was a single unit within which man moved, either as a spirit awaiting birth, as a human being, or as the spirit of one dead awaiting reincarnation. When they were tired they slept, and when they were hungry they ate; unless the need was urgent a task could be put aside and equally well taken up at dusk, in the morning, or when three floods had passed by. The division of time into regular units had no relevance to this way of life.

Unaware of the subtleties of this life, Burke's party travelled through Yandruwandha and Yawarrawarrka territory searching for somewhere to rest. They stopped at a large magnificent waterhole, surrounded by grass and teeming with game.

The Cooper is home to more than two hundred species of birds and thirteen types of fish. Down among the tangled tree roots are yabbies. The Aboriginal people made full use of these resources, trapping the fish and squelching their toes into the mud to feel for freshwater mussels or *thukali*. They were experts at mimicking giant emus, which they lured into woven nets. They ate lizards, marsupials and snakes, but plants and seeds formed the main part of their diet: mulga apples, succulent native figs, cucumbers, oranges, lemons and millet. There were coolibah seeds, pigweed and, most important of all, a small aquatic fern, known as nardoo, which provides seeds that can be ground into a paste and baked.

The Aboriginal people knew every inch of their land; they understood it. In the good seasons they ate a nourishing diet, and even during times of drought they could survive on what nature provided. But harvesting the local bush tucker demanded knowledge, skill and patience—qualities Burke lacked. He had come to conquer, not to learn.

The explorers' arrival must have been an astonishing experience for the Yandruwandha. Their land was being invaded by strange figures mounted on giant four-legged creatures that snorted and spat their way through the sandhills.

Today the descendants of the Yandruwandha have long been displaced from their traditional lands, but they still possess much of their tribal history and language. Stories of the explorers' stay on the Cooper have been passed down through the generations to Arran Patterson and his family. Arran's great-great-great grandfather Kimi was a young man when the expeditioners arrived at Cooper Creek in November 1860.

From the Yandruwandha perspective, the explorers behaved rudely. The waterholes along the Cooper were the equivalent of family homes and, as in most societies, Aboriginal people observed certain protocols when entering the territory of others.

The Yandruwandha watched in amazement as these strangers charged towards the water. They did not call the men 'whitefellas' but *pirti-pirti*, which means 'red fella'. Presumably Burke and his men were very sunburnt.

Wills was to notice that the Aborigines often gesticulated vigorously at them whenever they approached a waterhole. The explorers interpreted this as aggression but the Yandruwandha believe their ancestors may have been trying to communicate in sign language, which was used across Aboriginal Australia between different tribes. The Yandruwandha might have been asking, 'What are you doing?', 'Why are you here?' or, most importantly, 'How long are you going to stay?'

The Yandruwandha moved around so as not to exhaust a particular waterhole. Visitors who camped one or two nights could be tolerated, but what if they were to stay longer?

In fact the explorers were hardly a danger to the local food supplies. They did little more than take a few pot shots at ducks. Neither Burke nor Wills made any real effort to establish relations with the local people, despite the fact that the Yandruwandha often approached the explorers with offerings of fish or invitations to dances and ceremonies. All such advances were rejected, sometimes with a bullet in the air just to make sure the message was clear.

Burke may have had good reason to fear the Aboriginal people. Tales of their aggression were common in Melbourne and it was not unheard of for tribes to attack or kill settlers. He was also justified in worrying about theft, as much of his equipment was desirable to the locals. The Aborigines were more inclined to share property than the Europeans, and they expected that their gifts of fish and nardoo would be reciprocated with objects such as knives and axes. These were particularly sought-after, since the Aboriginal people had no metal of their own. But, although Burke tossed them a few trinkets, he ignored them as far as he could. Wills was equally dismissive:

A large tribe of blacks came pestering us to go to their camp and have a dance, which we declined. They were very trouble-some and nothing but the threat to shoot will keep them away; they are, however, easily frightened, and although fine-looking men, decidedly not of a war-like disposition…from the little we saw of them, they appear to be mean-spirited and contemptible in every respect.

While their actions may make sense when viewed in the context of their era when it was common to regard Aboriginal people as 'hostile savages' or 'ignorant blacks', Burke and Wills did not have the wit to realise that local people were the best judges of their land and its resources. Unlike explorers such as Gregory and Leichhardt, they lacked the vision to see beyond their prejudices. They were in too much of a hurry even to plunder the Cooper's most precious resource—the wisdom of its indigenous people.

While Burke and Wills explored the Cooper, William Wright made his way back to Menindee. His instructions to 'follow-up' the main party as fast as possible had seemed like a good plan out in the desert but when he rode back into town on 5 November 1860, Wright realised he was in an impossible situation.

Burke had plundered the best of the expedition, leaving Hermann Beckler in charge. Beckler had gone to nearby ranges on a botanical expedition. Ludwig Becker was sketching. Everyone else had lapsed into sullen indifference.

Wright was supposedly third-in-command, yet he had no written orders, dubious official status and little financial credibility. He lacked the natural authority of the ruling class and admitted later: 'I did not rightly know what to do.' Returning to find 'a mere station manager' was now in charge, Beckler refused to accept the appointment until it was confirmed in writing from Melbourne. This placed Wright in an untenable position. He was charged with carrying six tonnes of supplies a distance of 600 kilometres over arid terrain in summer with help from: a doctor who refused to accept his command (Herman Beckler); a lame artist (Ludwig Becker); the second blacksmith (Alexander MacPherson); a journalist (William Hodgkinson); and a dispirited sepoy (Belooch).

To mount a relief party, Wright calculated that he needed at least ten more strong horses, ten packsaddles and four bullocks for meat. The cost would top £400. Conscious that Burke's men were dependent on him Wright struggled to assemble the party. Then on 10 November news came that a horseman had ridden into town with urgent dispatches from Melbourne.

Trooper Lyons had been told to deliver his messages personally to Burke—and that was what he intended to do. Wright objected, arguing it was madness to rush off into the desert, but Lyons insisted. He carried news of John McDouall Stuart's retreat, as well as letters from the Exploration Committee urging Burke to make haste. The dispatches were all unnecessary. Burke knew about Stuart and he was already travelling as fast as he could towards the Gulf. Wright was at a disadvantage. His advice was sound—but to Lyons he was simply an uncooperative, illiterate sheep farmer without authority.

Burke had apparently promised Wright that he would stop at least twice on his way to the Cooper to rest his animals, so in the end Wright agreed that it might be possible to catch him up. He arranged with Lyons that once the messages were delivered, the trooper would bring back extra horses and camels to shuttle the rest of the supplies up to the Cooper. Wright instructed Alexander MacPherson to accompany Lyons and enlisted an Aboriginal tracker named Dick to show them the way. On 11 November, the trio set out.

Burke was restless. Taunted by the unknown terrain to the north of the Cooper, he took off alone, but returned without finding water or a way forward. On 16 November Wills took up the challenge, discovering that the land around the creek was divided into distinct types—none of them appealing to an aspiring explorer.

In some areas he found huge tracts of sandhill country. In others, the sand solidified into rock and Wills picked his way through the 'gibber plains' that had repulsed Charles Sturt. When the stones relented, open woodland took over. Wills returned to the depot disappointed. The waterholes were shrinking and there was no obvious way north.

Determined to try again, the surveyor took McDonough on his next trip. After setting out with three camels and travelling 130 kilometres, Wills and McDonough looked for water until they were exhausted. Thinking their camels were equally tired, they turned them loose. To their horror, the camels trotted off into the distance.

They were in a desperate position, stranded in the extreme heat with thirty-five litres of water in a leaking goatskin bag. Wills and McDonough abandoned all their equipment and began walking. Later, in a letter, Wills said, 'I can assure you there is nothing like a walk of this sort to make you appreciate the value of a drink of cold water.'

The men trudged fifteen kilometres when, by chance, they found stagnant pools to replenish their water bag. Over the next two days they marched another 115 kilometres, stopping for just a few hours to rest when the sun was at its height, and sipping the stinking black water. When the exhausted pair reached the Cooper, they had just half a litre of liquid left between them. Without Wills' determination, McDonough said, he would never have survived the journey.

At Wright's makeshift camp on the Darling, confusion reigned. In the unrelenting heat, petty disputes festered. No one bothered to fish or hunt, and the men lived on flour, sugar, tea and small amounts of dried beef. Their vitamin-deficient diet was already affecting their health. Both Becker and Beckler wrote several times to the committee, outlining their plight and requesting money and further instructions. Neither received any reply.

Wright bought in four bullocks to stockpile extra supplies of dried meat. The flesh was cut into long strips and strung between the trees. The fat was salted, wrapped in the skin of the dead beasts, buried for five days and then dug up and hung out to dry. The smell of rotting meat attracted clouds of flies. The men had to remove maggots from the meat each day.

Locals whispered that 'it was folly of Mr Wright to stop and let the season pass' just because he was waiting for his appointment to be approved. Wright was unrepentant. He maintained that he had taken all possible steps to resolve the situation by sending a formal request for confirmation to the Exploration Committee, along with some dispatches from Burke and Wills, by the first post after he returned from Torowoto.

Wright's packet of letters arrived in Melbourne on 3 December 1860. Burke's glowing descriptions of his progress towards the Cooper through excellent grazing country hardly reflected the expedition's disarray, but they were enough to seduce the committee. They overlooked the urgency of Wright's predicament. Despite further dispatches from Becker and Beckler dated 27 November they failed to reply—to confirm the station manager's appointment or issue any written orders.

Up at the Cooper, Burke and his men were overrun by a plague of native rats. They descended on the camp in swarms, devouring food supplies, boot leather and bedding. The rats scuttled over the men as they slept, gnawing their hair and chewing their toenails. Brahe trapped and shot three hundred in a single night. Exasperated, and in danger of losing more precious supplies, Burke decided to move on.

A few kilometres along the creek, he established a new camp. It was dominated by a magnificent coolibah tree nearly two centuries old. Its branches cast a welcome shadow over the sunbaked earth. The men slept, ate and cooked beneath its canopy.

Luxuriant grasses and shrubs thrived under the shade of the giant gums and flocks of budgerigars flit from branch to branch. But respite from the desert was brief. Just a few paces away from the water's edge, the temperature climbed. The earth was baked hard and then wrenched apart into a crinkled jigsaw. The trees diminished in size until they became stunted skeletal replicas scattered across the plains. All that was left was the earth and the sky.

Burke fretted. The arguments for staying at the Cooper until

Wright arrived were overwhelming. Wills' recent experiences proved that the route north was already perilous and from now on, the weather would only get hotter and the waterholes less reliable. Burke had no way of knowing how long it might take Wright to catch up with the rest of the supplies. A prudent leader would spend the next few weeks securing a line of communication and supply back to Menindee. A prudent leader would not rush off into the desert while so much uncertainty surrounded his back-up party.

But for Burke, the thought of waiting by the Cooper was more terrifying than the prospect of the desert. His honour depended on him reaching the Gulf before any other man. In any case, he reasoned, a delay would not necessarily be the safest option.

When Charles Sturt tried to penetrate the interior in January 1845, he became trapped, and sheltered in a small canyon for five months, waiting for cooler weather to release him. He and his men deteriorated in the grinding heat. Their hair stopped growing, their nails turned brittle and dropped out, and one man died in agony from scurvy.

Sturt returned to Adelaide strapped to his horse, almost blind, his gums bleeding and his legs black with scurvy. Burke was not keen to repeat Sturt's ordeal. Already, days by the Cooper were sliding together. At dawn there was a few brief hours of cool temperatures when the men could take the animals out to graze. But as the sun hit its stride, it became difficult to do anything at all. The men cowered in the shade swathed in netting.

Around late afternoon, a soft glow swept over the creek. For a brief, beautiful hour tranquillity returned, tempers were soothed.

97

At sunset the men stoked up the campfire and prepared supper. Afterwards, when the stories and jokes were exhausted, there was little for them to do except crawl into their bedrolls. Time belonged to another life. But Burke was not seduced.

Tiny black bushflies crawled into the men's eyes, ears, noses and mouths. When the mosquitoes came out, the men could sit in the choking smoke of the campfire or breathe freely and be bitten to death. Burke was losing patience. On 13 December, he wrote to the committee that 'the flies, mosquitoes and rats here render it a very disagreeable summer residence'. A rumble of thunder in the distance added to the feeling of suffocation.

For several days lightning scampered along the horizon. As Burke surveyed the dark clouds to the north, he contemplated the possibilities. Rain would fill the waterholes and make his crossing easier. Why wait any longer and use up more valuable supplies? His decision was inevitable. He would not wait for Wright.

In a dispatch to the committee, Burke justified his plan to leave the Cooper:

> I shall endeavour to explore the country to the north of it, in the direction of Carpentaria, and it is my intention to return here within three months at the latest. I did not intend to start so soon but we have had some severe thunderstorms lately with every appearance of heavy falls to the north; and as I have given the other route a fair trial, I do not wish to lose so favourable an opportunity.

The letter was disingenuous. Burke had never shown any real signs of wanting to consolidate his position on the Cooper, and if he had been genuinely expecting Wright to arrive, he could have sent Brahe south to help bring up the rest of his supplies.

Later that afternoon, Burke suggested to Brahe they go for a swim. As the two men floated in the creek's cool waters, Burke revealed his plan to leave with a flying party of just three men: William Wills, soldier John King and sailor Charley Gray. Then he said, 'I want someone to stay here and take the party back to the Darling if we don't return. I will give you command if you stop. It will be a distinction.'

Brahe was not convinced. The proposal sounded more like a nightmare than a promotion, especially as he too dreamed of crossing the continent. He refused to commit himself, and Burke was reluctant to force him. Wills had no such scruples. The next morning the surveyor called Brahe into his tent: 'We are in a fix,' he said. 'Someone must take charge here. You do it.'

Brahe remembered later that he 'hummed and hawed over the suggestion but just at that instant Burke came into the tent. Then Wills simply forced my hand. He said, "Brahe has offered to stay." "That's good," replied Burke, patting me on the shoulder, and so that settled it.' Brahe had already proved himself a capable member of the party, but he had never expected to take on such a great responsibility.

Apart from Brahe, three others would remain at the Cooper: Thomas McDonough (who was exhausted from his trip northwards and still in disgrace for losing the camels), William Patten, the blacksmith and, most surprisingly, Dost Mohomet. After thousands of pounds had been spent caring for the precious camels, the only skilled handler was to be left behind.

Burke reassured Brahe by telling him that Wright would have left Menindee on 15 November, and allowing around a month for the journey, he would be due to arrive any day. John King confirmed this assertion, saying that Burke 'expected Mr. Write Daily'.

But clearly Burke had not thought the situation through. How could Wright possibly be expected to procure extra horses, camels and jerked meat, then assemble a new party by 15 November? Then, there was the journey time from the Darling to the Cooper. Burke had made spectacular progress, completing the 600-kilometre march in just twenty-three days. But with summer advancing and the waterholes disappearing, he grossly underestimated Wright's task in retracing his steps. Obsessed with reaching the Gulf first, Burke had no credible contingency plans in case Wright failed to arrive, or in case he himself was away longer than expected.

Despite his ignorance of the terrain ahead, Burke was certain that he would be back in ninety days. According to Brahe, Burke asked him to wait for three months or until the supplies ran out. Thomas McDonough confirmed that Burke's instructions were to wait for 'three months and longer if he could'. Burke faced a return journey of around 3000 kilometres. To complete the trip within ninety days, his party would have to average at least thirty kilometres a day or else run out of food. It was a momentous task.

Wills took a more realistic view. He asked Brahe to wait for four months if he could. Nevertheless, Wills was still optimistic about the expedition's chances of success. As he prepared to leave the Cooper, he told his family he was in the very best of health, and even enjoying the limited diet of horseflesh, which was 'so delicious you would scarcely know it from beef'. Their 'travels so far had been very comfortable; in fact more like a picnic than a serious exploration'. There might be 'some little difficulties to

100   COOPER'S CREEK

contend with soon' but he predicted that the expedition would be back in Melbourne by August.

It was now twelve weeks since the explorers had left Melbourne and the party was about to split into three, with its supplies scattered from Menindee to Cooper Creek over a distance of 600 kilometres. Burke had backed himself into a tight corner. With only a small cache of supplies at the Cooper, the amount of food he could take to the Gulf was limited. He took supplies which, by Augustus Gregory's formula, were barely enough for four men for ninety days. He made no allowances for delays or the fact that the men would need extra food towards the end of the trek.

According to King, Burke proposed to shoot wild pigs and buffalo further north but, in light of the expedition's indifference to bush tucker so far, this seemed unlikely. His second strategy was more drastic. They would eat their transport. Valuable horses and camels would be sacrificed for food whenever necessary, even if it reduced the expedition's carrying capacity. There were now just twelve camels and thirteen horses left on the Cooper. Burke decided to take six camels and one horse to the Gulf and, since the animals might have to carry water as well, supplies and equipment were cut to a minimum. Apart from food, they took a few firearms, some spare clothing, a small number of scientific instruments, a bedroll and blankets for shelter. By any standards they were under-resourced for the journey ahead.

On the evening of 15 December, Burke handed William Brahe a sealed packet of papers, with instructions that they should be tossed into the creek unread if he failed to return. Wills also left behind a number of personal papers.

The next morning Burke lined up his men to say goodbye.

However erratic his leadership might have been, he still inspired the loyalty of his men and the whole party was overcome by the occasion. William Patten the blacksmith burst into tears and sobbed as Burke embraced each of his men.

Wills wrote: 'Sunday Dec 16, 1860. The two horses having been shod and reports finished, we started at forty minutes past six am for Eyres Creek, the party consisting of Mr Burke, myself, King, and Charley, having with us six camels, one horse, and three months provisions.' With no spare animals, the 'best equipped explorers ever to try for the Gulf' would be walking the whole way.

NINE

―――――

SHOOTING THE SUN

WITHOUT William Wills, there would be almost no record of the first European crossing of Australia. To begin with, he maintained his diary scrupulously. Later, as the trek began to take its toll, dates become muddled and days get lost in the battle for survival.

Overland navigation in 1860 was a laborious business. A surveyor needed a sextant, compasses, a telescope, a chronometer, a theodolite, and special measuring chains the length of a cricket pitch known as 'Gunter chains'. Wills travelled light. His most useful tool was a prismatic compass. The surveyor set his course, then kept to it as far as the terrain allowed. Rocky outcrops, rivers or boggy country meant detours and recalculations. Patches of open desert were so devoid of reference points that the party stuck to a predetermined bearing for days on end with nothing to aim for except the mirages hovering above the horizon.

To compile a proper map, Wills had to calculate the distance travelled each day. The most accurate methods were time-consuming. Some surveyors used a measuring wheel, others laid out their 20.1-metre Gunter chains end to end. Wills guessed his speed for a fixed distance and then extrapolated from that figure.

Latitude, the party's north–south position, was established by measuring the sun's altitude using a sextant and a pool of mercury enclosed in a vibration-proof box to create an artificial horizon. Several pairs of readings were necessary to make an accurate calculation and, despite years of practice, Wills found it tricky. 'In windy weather,' he complained, 'it is seldom possible to keep the mirror free from dust even for a few seconds and this so interferes with the readings of the spirit level that the altitudes taken with this horizon cannot be depended on.' Once altitude readings had been obtained, Wills used a special set of tables known as a nautical almanac to calculate his latitude.

Longitude, the party's east–west position, was established by comparing the local time with the time at a fixed point such as the Greenwich meridian. Since the earth revolves fifteen degrees every hour, if Wills knew the difference between the two times, he could calculate his longitude. This method was dependent on the accuracy of his chronometers, and in the 1860s it was a tall order to expect a watch to function without error through the desert.

As Charles Sturt and John McDouall Stuart had discovered, taking sun sightings in the desert was a painful process that ruined their eyesight. But Wills was also proficient at taking star sightings. If the night sky was clear he would spend at least an hour and a half working out the altitude and position of selected stars. Then he could calculate his latitude and his longitude without having to 'shoot the sun'.

In contrast to Wills' meticulous records, Burke's entire 'diary' consists of no more than 850 words in a leather-bound pocketbook, which is still smudged with red earth. The first few notes read:

> 16th December Left depot 65, followed by the creek.
> 17th The same.
> 18th The same. 67
> 19th We made a small creek, supposed to be Otta Era (?), or in the immediate neighbourhood of it. Good water. Camp 69.

20th Made a creek where we found a great many natives; they presented us with fish, and offered us their women. Camp 70.

Burke had always disliked paperwork. The walls of his Beechworth home were plastered with scraps of paper containing scribbled messages in English, French and German. A sign to visitors read: 'You are requested not to read anything on these walls, I cannot keep any record in a systematic manner, so I jot things down like this.'

Once they left Depot Camp 65, Burke, Wills, Gray and King found the first few days of the journey idyllic. Predictions of wastelands and Aboriginal warriors came to nothing as they led their camels through the gum trees alongside the Cooper. Even when they turned away from the creek, Wills found that between the sand dunes, the valleys were 'very pretty…and covered with fresh plants'.

William Brahe accompanied the party for the first day. The next morning, 17 December, Burke reiterated his belief that William Wright would be 'up in a few days', even instructing his new officer to catch him up with any messages if his back-up arrived soon. With this reassurance ringing in his ears, Brahe turned his horse around and headed back to camp, to await Burke's return. Neither he nor Burke had any idea of the extraordinary events taking place in Menindee, a few hundred kilometres to the south.

On 19 December, a ragged figure stumbled into view at the camp on the Darling. 'His face was sunken,' Hermann Beckler recalled, 'his tottering legs could hardly carry him, his feet were raw, his voice hoarse and whispering.'

It was Dick the Aboriginal tracker. He had left Trooper Lyons and Alexander MacPherson at Torowoto—home to the Wanji-walku people. The horses were lost or dead and the two white men were so weak they were unable to travel. Dick had walked for a week to save his companions, eating just two birds and a couple of lizards during his 300-kilometre journey.

Beckler offered to mount a rescue mission with Belooch and another Aboriginal guide named Peter. They set out with three

Charley Gray was well-liked and had proven bush skills. He was chosen by Burke to continue the expedition from Cooper Creek.

camels and a horse, pushing themselves as hard as they could to reach Lyons and MacPherson.

After a week of hard travelling, Beckler spotted MacPherson: 'He staggered towards us. For several minutes he was completely speechless, but finally he cried out, "Oh Doctor!", and tears streamed from his eyes.' Lyons was not far away. He was in better shape physically but 'had to be cheered up constantly by the others so that he did not despair completely'. They had lived for two weeks under an old horse blanket, scratching themselves raw from the mosquitoes.

MacPherson told Beckler they had suffered constantly from diarrhoea and vomiting as they tried to head north from Torowoto, and once their horses died, they had no choice but to retreat. Sometimes they were so thirsty they 'rinsed out their mouths with their own urine, and derived great relief from it'. It had taken all their strength to return to the waterholes, where Dick negotiated with the local Aborigines to bring them food, while he returned to Menindee. For a few days they received birds, snakes and the odd goanna before the local hunters moved on and they were reduced to gathering nardoo plants to grind into flour.

It would have been sensible for Beckler's rescue party to head back to Menindee all together, but by this time the doctor was carried away with his new role as an explorer. He decided to strike out for the nearby Goningberri Ranges with Peter, leaving the other three to walk back by themselves. The trio then argued over the choice of route and Belooch walked off by himself. Quite by chance, Beckler found him five days later wandering in circles, delirious and almost dead from thirst.

In all, the Lyons debacle had been nothing but a dangerous

waste of time. Three men had nearly died, four horses were gone and Wright had lost more valuable time—it was now two and a half months since Burke had left Menindee.

After Brahe departed a new routine settled over Burke's party. They tried to cover as much ground as possible before the sun took hold, so breakfast was postponed until mid-morning. Burke or Wills marched ahead carrying the compass followed by Gray leading Billy, and King bringing up the rear. After marching for two or three hours the men stopped for salted meat, damper and tea, often squatting behind the camels to shelter from the sun. Burke took all the major decisions regarding route and pace, but it was Wills who determined their course and plotted their position.

As the temperatures increased, the party would rest in the middle of the day and then travel late into the evening, continuing by moonlight if conditions allowed. Campsites were selected for their proximity to water, firewood, shade and good feed for the animals. Without tonnes of equipment, camps were quickly established. Within minutes of halting, King was tending the animals and Gray was collecting wood. It was his job to prepare the evening meal and bake the damper for the next day's journey. Once these tasks were complete, there was always equipment to mend, packs to reorganise and sores to bathe—no one relaxed for very long. Most nights, while supplies were plentiful, they ate a stew made with salt beef, poured over rice and bread, and finished off with a cup of tea and sugar.

It is unclear how much Burke contributed to the running of the camp. As leader, he was not expected to perform menial jobs, but it seems unlikely that he did nothing at all. Wills was always busy, taking meteorological observations, writing his journal and scientific records. After supper, the bedrolls were laid out, the campfire was stoked up to ward off the mosquitoes and each man lapsed into his own thoughts.

No one kept guard at night. Only Wills stayed awake to take star sightings and finish his navigational calculations. He was the only one of the party with any idea where they were.

The Exploration Committee had asked Burke to mark his route 'as permanently as possible, by leaving records, sowing seeds, building cairns at as many points as possible'. The expedition leader was careless about such obligations but, every evening, King took a knife and hacked away the bark of a tree to engrave the letter 'B', followed by the camp number. Once the tracks of the horses and camels were washed away, these small engravings became the only evidence of the first European journey across Australia.

The dynamics of this small group were finely balanced. Each man was dependent on the skills of the others, so personal quirks and weaknesses stood out. In practical terms, Wills was a more capable leader than Burke, but the Irishman had a charisma that either infuriated or inspired. The two men were complete opposites in most respects, yet they developed a relationship of 'affectionate intimacy', with Burke referring to his deputy as 'My dear boy'. As the days passed, the four men seemed to settle down well and the journey north was free of the hostility that had torn the expedition apart on the way to Menindee. In particular, twenty-two-year-old John King was distinguishing himself as a versatile and capable member of the party. Small, quiet and shy, he was an unlikely explorer.

John King grew up during the Great Famine in the village of Moy, County Tyrone. To ensure he escaped poverty, his father (himself a soldier) enrolled him at a military college in Dublin. At the age of fourteen King was a member of the British army.

A year later King was posted to India. In 1857, he was stationed in Peshawar at the height of the Indian Mutiny. Soon afterwards he went on leave for sixteen months after contracting 'fever of a bad type', a complaint that was probably exacerbated by the initial stages of consumption. King was convalescing in Karachi in 1859 when he met George Landells. The camel trader was impressed with the young man's ability to speak the languages of the sepoy camel handlers, and suggested that King sign up for a grand expedition across Australia. King purchased his discharge and joined Landells on the trek through India to take the camels back to Australia. By the time they reached Melbourne, Landells was more convinced than ever of King's worth and persuaded Burke to hire him at a salary of £120 per year.

During the power struggle that erupted on the way to Menindee, King might have been expected to sympathise with Landells, but there was never any hint of him taking sides or incurring Burke's wrath. Calm and reserved, with a strong sense of duty, King melted into the background and got on with his job. His reward was a place in the forward party.

With King in charge of the camels, the rest of the camp work fell to ex-sailor Charley Gray. A tall bear-like man in his forties, his employer Thomas Dick described him as a 'stout and hearty' worker, who got drunk just once a month when he received his wages. With his easygoing personality, Gray seemed to get on well with everyone on the expedition. Now, with his sinewy arms covered in tattoos of mermaids and anchors, Gray was about to embark on the first overland crossing of Australia.

In the first week the expedition averaged around twenty-five kilometres a day. Burke and his men were doing well. As the terrain grew harsher, they displayed an uncanny ability to discover the most fertile strips of land, in areas where just a kilometre either way might make the difference between finding water or dying of thirst. Their first stroke of good fortune was to traverse an area 100 kilometres above the Cooper, known as Coongie Lakes—one of the richest ecological sites in Australia, important to many Aboriginal groups but principally to the Yawarrawarrka people, who know the area as Kayityirru.

Coongie's Aboriginal inhabitants were astounded by the strangers who set up camp at their waterholes, but they expressed neither fear nor hostility. Wills found the local people remarkably welcoming:

> There was a large camp of not less than forty or fifty blacks near where we stopped. They brought us presents of fish, for which we gave them some beads and matches. These fish we found to be a most valuable addition to our rations. They were the same kind as we had found elsewhere, but finer.

Later, both Burke and Wills mention that the local tribesmen offered them women, according to their custom. These invitations were rejected in disgust.

Wills was often surprised that they didn't see more Aborigines, unaware that the party was constantly monitored by a network of well-camouflaged messengers.

On several occasions Burke and Wills tried to persuade

Aboriginal men to guide them, although they did not resort to the brutal tactics of later explorers such as David Carnegie. He would often hunt and capture Aboriginal people, then tie them to a tree until thirst forced them to point the way to the nearest billabong. Wills offered beads and mirrors as enticements but there was no time to win anyone's trust and his attempts failed.

On Christmas Eve, nearly 200 kilometres from the Cooper, they reached a campsite Wills described as their most beautiful so far:

> We took a day of rest on Gray's Creek, to celebrate Christmas. This was doubly pleasant, as we had never…anticipated finding such a beautiful oasis in the desert. Our camp was really an agreeable place for we had all the advantages of food and water attending a position on a large creek or river, and were at the same time free of the annoyances of the numberless ants, flies and mosquitoes.

The party left Gray's Creek at 4 a.m. on Christmas Day, but lethargy soon overtook them. Burke recorded: 'At two pm, Golah Singh [a camel] gave some very decided hints about stopping and lying down under the trees. Splendid prospect.' Every hour of rest was a luxury. The party was still travelling too slowly and using up too much food.

The forward terrain was unpredictable. There were stretches of easy walking across drying claypans and lightly timbered plains, but there were also large tracts of boggy ground and kilometres of monotonous red dunes. Even so, the horrors of Sturt's Stony Desert were never fully realised. The simmering rubble appeared only in patches, leaving Wills sceptical of their fearsome reputation: 'We camped at the foot of a sand-ridge jutting out on to the stony desert. I was disappointed although not altogether surprised that the latter was nothing more than the stony rises we had met with before, only on a larger scale and not quite as undulating.' The camels coped better on the rugged sections than expected, while the men stumbled along, never quite hitting their stride.

They sweated profusely and if they worked too hard their heads began to pound and they felt dizzy. Disturbed vision and stomach cramps followed. Dehydration was a constant danger. In severe conditions, when a person sweats up to two litres per hour, it becomes almost impossible for the gut to absorb enough water to keep up. The explorers compounded the problem by marching for many hours without drinking, then guzzling large amounts of liquid once they had stopped. This was the worst way to rehydrate. Their digestive systems couldn't cope and they felt bloated and sick.

Burke and his men carried about three and a half litres with them per day, yet they would have needed at least fifteen litres just to replenish what they were sweating away. Although they always had sufficient water each evening, they must have been danger-ously thirsty throughout most of the day's march. Dehydration has a devastating effect on the body's physical performance. The explorers were pushing their bodies to the limit day after day. It was an extraordinary demonstration of stamina and determination but the cumulative effects were inescapable.

Mentally, such journeys are just as testing. 'Each day,' John King scribbled towards the end of December, 'we had to face the Desert again.' Keeping a sense of perspective while marching becomes a conjuring trick of the mind and people have to find their own way of coping.

Burke and Wills were stoic about their physical circumstances. By now they were sometimes achieving sixty kilometres in a single march. If anything, the relative ease with which they coped during the early stages of the journey belied the magnitude of the task ahead. For now, luck was running in Burke's favour. It was Christmas, and the explorers were about to receive a geographical gift that would take them all the way to the Gulf of Carpentaria.

TEN

BENEATH THE VEIL

THE revelation occurred as Burke's party toiled through the sandhills. In the open sun, the men clawed their way up the ramparts as the grit slithered away beneath them. They tried to keep to the meshes of vegetation that anchored the sand—but marching through the clumps of spinifex was like striding through razor blades and their trousers hung in rags around their bloody ankles. Marching parallel to the hills, down in the claypans, was easier. But the danger was that by sticking to the low-lying ground, they might miss creeks or lagoons just one sandhill to the left or right. It would be easy to die just a few hundred feet from a water source.

A party could wander for weeks, as Sturt's did, and find nothing, but Burke and Wills hit the jackpot on 27 December, just south of the present-day town of Birdsville. They climbed yet another dune and moments later were gazing down over a floodplain. They had found a branch of the Diamantina River. If they had veered any further to the west, they would have found themselves entangled in the Simpson Desert—the world's largest parallel dune system.

Finding the Diamantina was the key to reaching the Gulf of Carpentaria. It would lead them towards the Georgina River system, and from there almost directly north to the coast.

The explorers were not the only people taking advantage of

the river. Many tribes, including the Wangkamana, the Yarluyandi, the Wangkangurru, the Mithaka and the Karuwali, lived in the area. Some were not only brave enough to approach but generous enough to point out the best billabongs as well.

It was now nearly three weeks since the party had left Depot Camp 65. Despite the plentiful grass Wills realised that the camels were 'greatly in need of rest'. While camels can travel up to 100 kilometres in a day, they cannot sustain this for long periods. It was a worrying sign, especially as they had at least 1200 kilometres to go to reach the north coast.

In Burke's defence, he had probably been taken in by the claims Landells had made to impress the committee. He surged on, taking no rest days, managing to average thirty to forty kilometres a day. A rare diary entry for 5 January 1861 reveals that the pace was beginning to tell on him as well:

> Water at Wills' or King's Creek. It is impossible to say the time were up, for we had to load the camels, to pack and feed them, to watch them and the horse, and to look for water, but I am satisfied that the frame of man never was more severely taxed.

As the explorers trekked towards the Georgina River system they found that the country was improving 'by the yard'. The grass was abundant and the riverbanks were smothered with yellow and white 'poached egg daisies'. They soon reached an area near the present-day outpost of Boulia. On 7 January, one of the pack camels rolled, slightly damaging some of Wills' instruments. He worried that the accident might affect the accuracy of his navigational calculations.

As they followed a large creek, now known as the Burke River, the vegetation was changing; the dark gnarled coolibahs were giving way to smooth silver ghost gums. Flocks of pelicans were reappearing along the waterways. The worst of the desert was behind them and the tropics were close at hand.

Until the failure of Trooper Lyons' mission, William Wright clung to the idea that Burke would send back extra pack animals. But when Dick returned alone, he realised it was not to be. Exasperated by the delay, the journalist William Hodgkinson wrote out a dispatch dictated by Wright and set off for Melbourne on 22 December. He arrived at John Macadam's house on New Year's Eve.

The message raised the fear that Burke might have pushed on without waiting for his extra supplies. According to Wright, there was now 'the most serious apprehensions to the safety of himself and his party'. Macadam held an emergency meeting where the committee expressed surprise that Wright wasn't on his way to the Cooper. It confirmed Wright's appointment and authorised him to spend £400. By 9 January Hodgkinson was back in Menindee.

Meanwhile, John McDouall Stuart was preparing to head north again. To the delight of Adelaide, Stuart's journey had revealed stretches of the 'finest pastoral country' in among the 'barren tracts and dismal ranges'. 'We are not, after all,' cried the *Register*, 'the occupants of a mere strip of country, shut in by the sea on one hand and the impassable desert on the other. There opens before us a new world, with new fields for our enterprise and new outlets for our industry.' That Stuart had proved the 'empty interior' to be full of indigenous people with established cultural and social networks was ignored. Australia was 'terra nullius'—a land owned by no one.

The Scotsman was not in the best of health to mount a renewed attack on the Australian interior. He had returned with advanced scurvy, which turned his legs black and inflicted such pain that he 'almost wished death would come and release me from my torture'. Sun sightings had destroyed his eyesight and left him with periods of double vision and blindness. Yet as Burke had predicted, Stuart began to assemble a new expedition at once. It took three frustrating months for him to gather nine men, forty horses and supplies.

Stuart ran a very different style of expedition from Burke. He travelled hard each day but rested every Sunday. He selected his staff based on personal knowledge and previous experience. Discipline was harsh but, judging from the loyalty of his men, it was also fair. Later on, Stuart compiled a written set of rules, which governed his subsequent expeditions, some of which were:

> No horses are to be abused, kicked or struck about the head. Sore backs etc are to be attended to after unsaddling. No horse to be put out of a walk except of necessity.
>
> When anything is used it must be packed up in the same manner as found and returned to the place whence it came.
>
> No one is to leave the line of march without my knowledge or that of the officer in charge. When leaving camp no one must go without arms and ammunition.
>
> No one is to fire on the natives without orders unless in self-defence.
>
> No swearing or improper language shall be allowed.
>
> Each man must sleep with his arms at his side, and in case

of attack from the natives a half-circle to be formed three feet apart.

His strict routine meant each expedition ran like clockwork. The horses and their packsaddles were numbered and divided into groups. Each animal learned its place and lined up automatically every morning and evening in the correct order.

Unlike Burke, Stuart never divided his party unless absolutely necessary and he fretted about anyone separated from the main group. He relied heavily on his two most trusted officers, Francis Thring and William Kekwick. Thring and his horse Gloag had an uncanny ability to find water which saved the party in many desperate situations.

On Friday 11 January 1861, Stuart's party set out. Perched on top of the leading horse was the expedition's pet dog Toby, who refused to stay behind. Conditions at the beginning of the journey were severe. It was mid-summer and many of the best waterholes had dried out. 'Poor little Toby' was the first casualty, upsetting even Stuart, who recorded that his death was 'regretted by us all'. The men battled on, the intense glare torturing Stuart in particular. As they headed towards the MacDonnell Ranges, there were periods when he could hardly see at all.

On 11 January, Burke's party rose as usual at dawn, but the daylight seemed sluggish in arriving. An eerie gloom enveloped the camp, unsettling the camels and mystifying the explorers. It was Wills who realised there was an eclipse. They 'made good the day's journey, the moderation of the mid-day heat, which was only about 86 deg., greatly assisting us'.

Even when the eclipse had passed, the conditions remained

favourable. 'The country traversed has the most verdant and cheerful aspect,' wrote Wills, there is an 'abundance of feed and water everywhere.'

Wills' diary is an excellent indicator of the expedition's morale. When the going was good, his entries contain enthusiastic descriptions of the surrounding landscape. When it was tough, he lapses into silence, often for days at a time. On Sunday 13 January, a ragged line began to tear at the horizon. Small, vicious outcrops of sharp stone started to replace the lush grasslands.

It was Wills' last entry for six days.

It was the Standish and Selwyn ranges—a bewildering labyrinth of gorges crisscrossed with sharp slaty ridges and steep slopes of loose scree—that caused the sharp break in Wills' diary. Wills' map shows that the men tried to scrabble their way westwards through the range, but were forced to turn back and try a route further to the east. For once it was Burke who described their ordeal:

> 18th January. Still on the ranges, the camels sweating profusely from fear.

> 20th January. I determined today to go straight at the ranges, and so far the experiment has succeeded well. The poor camels sweating and groaning, but we gave them a hot bath in Turner's Creek, which seemed to relieve them very much. At last through—the camels bleeding, sweating and groaning.

It wasn't just the terrain that was dangerous. Burke and Wills were deep inside Kalkadoon territory—one of the fiercest Aboriginal tribes who later resisted European settlement by mounting successful guerrilla-style campaigns against miners, pastoralists and policemen.

The men soon realised that they were being watched from the mountains. 'We found here numerous indications of blacks been here,' remarked Wills, 'but we didn't see them.' Twenty years later, a miner out prospecting for copper got to know some of the Kalkadoon tribal elders. They told him that the younger men had planned to kill the explorers but realised that the men were accompanied by giant roaring beasts, which they assumed must be supernatural. They retreated and watched the party from high up in the cliffs.

Ignorant of the drama taking place around them, the explorers were walking only eight or ten kilometres a day. Wills diary does not resume in earnest until 27 January when he noted with relief that the party had now crossed the Selwyn Ranges.

As the terrain began to flatten out, the expedition skirted the site of the present-day town of Cloncurry (named after Burke's cousin Lady Cloncurry) and headed north-west. Several falsely marked trees and vandalised campsites mean there is now confusion about whether the party followed the Cloncurry or the Corella rivers, but Wills' diary suggests that the Corella is more likely. This route led them north until the end of January. Then, the party crossed Augustus Gregory's 1856 east–west track along the Top End of Australia, approximately 200 kilometres from the coast.

The expedition had fulfilled its official responsibility to explore the country between the Cooper and Gregory's track. Burke could have turned back with honour. Even more importantly, the party had reached what modern explorers refer to as 'Drop Dead Day' or the 'PNR' (point of no return). On 30 January Burke should have turned south. He was halfway through his allotted schedule of ninety days and the party was using up its supplies faster than anticipated. Every day spent travelling further north decreased the odds of survival.

Did the more circumspect Wills ever raise the subject of retreat? Did King or Gray ever realise they were in danger or petition their leader to turn back? There was never any doubt that Burke would press on past the point of no return.

Crossing the Selwyn Ranges plunged the expedition into the oppressive heat of the tropics. They were in what is now known as the Gulf country, an area of flat terrain governed by a climate of two seasons: the 'dry' between May and November and the 'wet' between December and April. The monsoon was late, so they were travelling in the 'build-up' just before the rainy season, when the humidity climbs and the air thickens until it is almost difficult to breathe.

The temperature no longer fell at night and the men lay on their bedrolls, tossing and turning. Food rotted and leather harnesses grew furry with mould. The camels were fretful and listless. Burke was pushing the animals too hard and, at the beginning of February, disaster struck. Golah, a large bull, clambered down into a creek but couldn't get back out. After pushing the exhausted beast for five kilometres along the creek bed, the explorers were forced to abandon him.

Burke, Wills and King had no choice but to redistribute the loads and continue with their remaining five camels. Soon afterwards they found a new waterway heading north. It was the beginnings of the Flinders River. The silty sluggish waters were broken every now and then by turtles poking their heads through the algae and occasionally by a crocodile floating just under the surface.

After Golah's accident, Wills' diary is once again silent until 9 February. Since leaving Melbourne, Burke, Wills, Gray and King had travelled for more than five months with hardly a rest day—a 2500-kilometre journey through bogs, deserts and mountain ranges in frost, hail, rain, windstorms, sandstorms, heat and overpowering humidity. Now, as they followed the Flinders River, their goal was close.

It is tempting to imagine the explorers scenting the salt in the air, climbing a small rise and seeing a white sandy beach falling away into the sparkling ocean. But the reality was so different.

As Burke and Wills neared the north coast, the countryside closed in around them. The thickets of small trees grew so dense it was difficult to force a way through. As the ground became wetter, the camels could go no further on the boggy ground. The men unloaded their gear and made camp at a small waterhole on the junction of the Bynoe and Flinders rivers.

It is not recorded who first noticed the bitter saline taste of the water from the creek at Camp 119 or realised that twice a day, the murky liquid rose and fell a few centimetres, but these clues confirmed that Burke's party had just about reached its objective. The ocean could not be far away. By this stage, not even Wills knew exactly where they were. He had plotted their route towards the Albert River, which was actually 100 kilometres away to the west.

This dank muddy campsite was as far as Gray and King ever reached. Leaving them to care for the camels, Burke and Wills set off into the territory of the Yappar Aboriginal people to find the ocean.

They toiled through land 'so soft and rotten, a horse, with only a saddle and about twenty-five pounds on his back, could scarcely walk over it', through 'quicksand' for several miles before finding a path 'formed by the blacks':

> About half a mile further we came across a blackfellow, who was coiling by a campfire whilst his gin and his picaninny were yabbering alongside. We stopped for a short time to take out some of the pistols that were on the horse, and that they might see us before we were so near as to frighten them. Just after we stopped, the black got up to stretch his limbs, and after a few seconds looked in our direction. It was very amusing to see the way in which he stared, standing for some time as if he thought he must be dreaming, and then, having signalled to the others, they dropped on their haunches and shuffled off in the quietest manner possible…
>
> Proceeding on our course across the marsh, we came to a channel through which the sea water enters. Here we passed three blacks, who, as is universally their custom, pointed out to us, unasked, the best part down.

Burke and Wills managed only a few kilometres more. The ground disintegrated into a tangle of impassable mangrove swamps. The journey north was over. They did not see the ocean.

Burke wrote later in his notebook: 'At the conclusion of the report, it would be well to say that we reached the sea, but we could not obtain a view of the open ocean although we made every endeavour to do so.' Wills made no diary entry at all.

The explorers had made it to within twenty kilometres of the coast.

Burke and Wills left no monument to mark their historic crossing. There was no moment of exhilaration, no time to sit and contemplate victory. Instead, exhausted and demoralised, they turned and waded back through swampy water towards Camp 119. Back in the small clearing, King and Gray had kept themselves busy catching a few fish and keeping watch over the camp. King spent several hours marking a circle of trees with the letter B, the only evidence that the expedition had reached this far north.

Burke reassured himself that the committee would be 'quite satisfied' that he had completed his mission 'as far as it was necessary'. And he could take some comfort in knowing that he had beaten John McDouall Stuart across the continent, even if the culmination of the journey had yielded little useful information about the north coast. Now he must retrace his steps to the Cooper, 1500 kilometres to the south.

As the men contemplated their return, the weather deteriorated. So far the monsoon had been light but now the rain fell in torrents. The mood was grim. It had taken nearly two months to reach the Gulf from the depot camp, yet Burke had told William Brahe to wait just three months before considering them 'perished', or 'on their way to Queensland'. Wills must have been remembering his whispered entreaty to Brahe to hang on for four months if he could. Suddenly the expedition was no longer a race for glory. It was a fight for survival.

At Menindee, William Wright was busy trying to break in ten horses. Training the horses was a mammoth task and the expedition was delayed for a further two weeks. In the end it was more than three months after Burke's departure from Menindee before the back-up party was ready to leave. It was 26 January 1861 when William Wright and his men finally set out.

In the meantime, William Brahe and his men had been stranded in the middle of the continent, sitting in the shade of the large coolibah tree on the banks of Cooper Creek. The men were finding it difficult to cope with the insidious effects of boredom and inactivity.

For the first few weeks after Burke left Brahe, Patten, McDonough and Dost Mohomet were reasonably busy. They built a stockade to store their equipment and ammunition, and established a routine to take care of the animals. Each day, one man would take out the horses to graze, while another watched over the camels. It was tiring, tramping up to ten or fifteen kilometres along the creek looking for the best fodder.

The other two men stayed behind, one on guard and the other gathering firewood, collecting water and baking endless loaves of damper. Apart from their periodic encounters with the local people, each day was crushingly similar to the last—a dislocation from reality—trapped on the creek cut off on all sides by a desert that shimmered in the raging heat.

The Aboriginal tribes were fascinated but perplexed by their new neighbours. They attempted to make contact by bringing presents of fish and nets but they also had a tendency to take whatever they could find lying around the camp. Their ability to appear from nowhere and steal everything from tin cans to saddles made Brahe jumpy. Outnumbered, in hostile territory, he couldn't afford to take risks. Under such stress, the cultural divide between the parties was just too great. No meaningful communication was ever established and relations swung between tolerance and hostility. The confrontations with the Aborigines had a paralysing effect on Dost Mohomet. He had been the major supplier of ducks and fish from the creek, but he became so scared that he refused to go out hunting at all.

When Brahe wasn't checking over his shoulder, he was scanning the horizon looking for William Wright. He remained convinced that the relief party would appear at any moment. But the sun rose and fell each day, and still no one came. Brahe was perplexed. By March, his thoughts began to turn north instead of south. He knew that Burke would go 'all out' for the coast, but he also knew that the party only had rations for three months. When April arrived, Brahe rode to the top of the surrounding hills each day to look out for any signs of Burke's return. There was nothing.

The four castaways lapsed into a lethargic mechanical routine. Fear began to penetrate the monotony. Patten was complaining that his gums were sore and that his legs ached. Brahe's party did not possess detailed knowledge of scurvy but they were familiar with 'barcoo rot', a scurvy-like disease that afflicted stockmen on an inadequate diet. They also knew that without fresh food barcoo rot could result in an agonising death.

All around them the sun melted the horizons and the ground throbbed in the heat. They huddled under the shade of the giant coolibah—and waited.

ELEVEN

TURNING SOUTH

THE journey to the Gulf had been a great achievement—far in excess of anything Burke's critics had predicted. But it had been achieved at great cost. An audit of the remaining supplies on 12 February 1861 revealed the four men had used up nearly three-quarters of their rations. It seemed unlikely that they would have the time or the energy to supplement their food with bush tucker so Burke ordered that each man's daily ration should be cut in half.

As fatigue set in, King took charge of the camp. On the morning of 13 February 1861, he packed the last of the supplies. Then Burke, Wills, Gray and King turned south.

Conditions were miserable from the start. During the first week they managed just six or seven kilometres a day as daily thunderstorms tore open the skies.

Navigation was easy, they simply retraced their steps from camp to camp. On Saturday 2 March, after battling south for two and a half weeks, they found Golah waiting for them near a creek. The camel had worn a path along the bank, walking up and down looking for his companions. The effort had reduced him to a virtual skeleton but he began to eat as soon as the others arrived. The temperature combined with the humidity sapped their energy. Even Wills' customary optimism deserted him:

> The evening was most oppressively hot and sultry—so much so that the slightest exertion made one feel as if he were in a state

of suffocation. The dampness of the atmosphere prevented any evaporation, and gave one a helpless feeling of lassitude that I have never experienced to such an extent.

Day and night ceased to matter. They started at 2 a.m. or 2 p.m., or whenever they could muster the energy to carry on.

One ritual dominated each day's proceedings. Morning and evening, the explorers would line up with their backs to Burke, waving away the flies until he told them to call out a number. One by one the men turned around to claim their designated plate and remove the handkerchief that covered it. Underneath they found a measure of flour or a few sticks of rotting meat. This pitiful process was all they had to look forward to each day.

Despite traversing fertile country, they still made little effort to utilise the natural foods that thrived all around them. Wills only managed to shoot one pheasant-like bird, which proved to be 'all feathers and claws'.

The only living food source they exploited was portulac, a fleshy plant that tasted like spinach when boiled. It soon became a staple part of their diet. Wills declared it an 'excellent vegetable'. Packed with vitamins A and C, it was all that stood between them and scurvy.

On 3 March, for the first (and only) time on their journey, they tried a more exotic form of bush food when Charley Gray rode over a large snake. Wills wrote later:

We thought it was a log until he struck it with the stirrup iron. We then saw that it was an immense snake, larger than any that I have ever before seen in a wild state…The weight was eleven pounds and a half.

That night they dined on python steaks. Wills christened that night's stopover 'Feasting Camp' but he spoke too soon—the reptile had a disastrous effect on the intestines of Burke and Gray:

> Mr Burke felt very unwell, having been attacked by dysentery since eating the snake. He now felt giddy, and unable to keep his seat.

The next day things improved. After several painful and undignified hours, Burke and Gray seemed to be regaining their strength, the weather lightened and the humidity dropped bringing 'a beneficial effect to all'. Relief came too late for Golah. He had never recovered from his time alone on the creek and he could no longer keep up. Inexplicably, Burke and Wills didn't shoot him for meat but abandoned him once more in the bush.

As the hardships of the journey took their toll, it was inevitable that tensions should begin to appear within the party. The problems began with the decline of Charley Gray. His jovial personality was disappearing, and he began to lag behind in silence.

Gray had grumbled about headaches on the journey north and now he complained of leg and back pains as well. He began to weaken rapidly. 'Mr Burke almost recovered,' Wills wrote on 7 March, 'but Charley is again very unwell, and unfit to do anything; he caught cold last night through carelessness in covering himself.'

Wills' attitude seems callous—but perhaps it was a sign that, in order to survive, each man was lapsing into his own constricted world. The journey was draining their reserves of compassion and a sick man was a huge burden on such a small party. With the

Selwyn Ranges looming once more on the horizon, second time around, Wills found a better route through them and the party were soon 'safely over the most dangerous part of our journey'.

Wills makes no special mention of 15 March 1861 in his diary but he must have known the significance of the date. It was three months since they had left the Cooper. Their time was up. According to Burke's instructions, Brahe was now authorised to return to Menindee if he chose. Yet Burke, Wills, Gray and King were still 1100 kilometres from the depot camp. Would Brahe wait any longer? Would he hang on for four months as Wills asked?

To speed things up, Burke reduced their rations once more and rummaged through the packs for superfluous equipment which was left behind.

As the days dragged past, and Wills found it harder to maintain his diary, it was often the camp names that told the story of their journey. 'Humid Camp' was 21 March, followed by 'Muddy Camp', and 'Mosquito Camp'.

After crossing the Selwyn Ranges, Burke and King began to complain of leg and back pains, but it was still Gray who was causing the most concern. On Monday 25 March, the grim unity that had sustained the party for nearly six weeks since they left the Gulf evaporated. That evening, Wills wrote:

> After breakfast…I found Gray behind a tree eating skilligolee. He explained that he was suffering from dysentery, and had taken the flour without leave. Sent him to report to Mr Burke, and went on. He, having got King to tell Mr Burke for him, was called up and received a good thrashing. There is no knowing to what extent he has been robbing us. Many things have been found to run unaccountably short.

King remembered the incident differently. He said that Gray was terrified of admitting his crime to Burke. The sailor begged him to report the incident on his behalf. King agreed and then stood to one side as Burke lost his temper:

> Mr Burke called him, and asked him what he meant by stealing the stores, and asked him if he did not receive an equal share which of course, he could not deny; Mr Burke then gave him several boxes on the ear with his open hand, and not a sound thrashing, as Mr Wills states; Mr Wills was at the other camp at the time, and it was all over when he returned. Mr Burke may have given him six or seven slaps on the ear.

Under normal circumstances, Gray's crime was trivial. To four starving men, it was a major offence. Trust had disappeared. From that moment on, Gray was not allowed near the packs without supervision—he had betrayed them all. There were no more friendly mentions of 'Charley' in Wills' diary. From now on he was only ever referred to as Gray.

It must have been a difficult atmosphere as the men loaded up the remaining supplies the next morning. The weather provided the only relief. The monsoon began to lose its influence and the lush tropical vegetation gave way once more to spinifex and mulga scrub.

The terrain was now so changeable that the men did not know what trial they might face next. As the stone country reappeared, the rocks tore at their tattered boots. Out on the open plains, the sense of space was now a terrible reminder of how far they had to go.

Rations were critically low. Burke had always intended to shoot his camels for food if he had to. Since it was now a toss-up as to who would collapse first—the men or the animals—Burke decided it was time to sacrifice the weakest camel. On 30 March, Boocha was led away from the rest of the herd and shot. His throat was cut, his skin peeled away and strips of meat were carved from the carcass to be dried.

All four men were suffering from chronic exhaustion. The pains in their legs and backs were almost certainly symptoms of beri-beri or Vitamin B deficiency. Their biggest problem was an overall lack of food. The men's bodies were gradually beginning to digest themselves.

Gray was deteriorating fastest. He now did little but complain of pains and weakness in his legs and back. Wills had little sympathy. On 8 April, as the party retraced their steps near the Diamantina River, he wrote: 'Halted fifteen minutes to send for Gray who gammoned he couldn't walk.' Soon afterwards the sailor collapsed. From now on he was another encumbrance to be carried by his weakened companions. In a brief moment of lucidity, as he was lifted onto a camel and strapped into place, he asked Wills to give his small cache of personal belongings to Police Superintendent Foster at Bendigo.

Only Billy was in worse condition. The next day, the horse's legs buckled and he sank into the sand. Given Burke's sentimental streak, it must have been difficult to shoot him. Wills on the other hand was practical. 'As we were running short of food of every description ourselves,' he noted, 'we thought it best to secure his flesh at once. We found it healthy and tender, but without the slightest trace of fat in any portion of the body.'

The meat was a welcome relief, but no amount of Billy-stew seemed to be enough to reinvigorate them. Gray was becoming a heavier burden. Nearing Coongie Lakes, with 150 kilometres to go to the Cooper, he continued to worsen. Wills became convinced that Gray's problems were his own fault. He declared that 'the man's constitution was gone through drink, as he had lived in a public house at Swan Hill, and I have heard since that he drunk very heavily there'.

On 17 April, nine days after Wills had accused Gray of shamming, the sailor proved him wrong. Wills' diary entry is terse: 'This morning, about sunrise, Gray died. He had not spoken a word distinctly since his first attack, which was just as we were about to start.' According to King, Gray's pain had grown worse until he became delirious and unable to speak. He spent his last few days strapped semi-comatose to a camel.

It was Burke who gave the order to halt and give Gray a decent burial. Fighting his own exhaustion, King took a shovel and scraped out a hole in the dirt. Despite Gray's emaciated state, it was all his companions could do to carry the body to the grave. There was no burial service. Charley Gray the sailor ended his days about as far from the sea as it was possible to be. The digging took up an entire day.

The next morning everything except the absolute essentials was discarded. The situation was still desperate, but without Gray they might make better progress. Provided their strength held out, relief was not far away. A surge of optimism returned and they even talked of coming back in a few days to pick up the things they had abandoned. The depot was close enough to allow thoughts of a victorious homecoming to sustain them during the final hours of the journey.

Surely William Brahe had hung on? Backed up by Wright's

party and its fresh supplies the depot on the Cooper would be substantial. How surprised Brahe and his companions would be to see this ragged trio stumble in from the unknown. The dishevelled explorers could almost hear the shouts of welcome.

Such was their confidence that on 20 April, the trio devoured the last of Billy. Wills knew the depot was not far away and they would need all the strength they could muster for one last effort. According to King they were still 'very weak' and the camels were so exhausted that 'they were scarcely able to get along', but that day they made it to within fifty kilometres of the depot. One way or another, tomorrow's march would be the last.

As the sun rose on 21 April 1861, the men knew that surviving the day's ordeal would be a matter of willpower. To begin with they tried to save the camels but, in the final desperate hours, they found they could stagger no further. It was early evening as they neared Cooper Creek. Wills had navigated for nearly 1500 kilometres since leaving the coast and he had returned them to the same waterhole they had left just over four months earlier.

Burke rode on ahead. Dusk was settling around the water-holes. Several times, he yelled out in excitement to the others. There were tents ahead—he was sure of it. Exhilaration surged through the tiredness and he began to shout out greetings to Brahe, McDonough and Patten. When they didn't answer, Burke bellowed a mighty 'coo-ee' into the bush.

There was no reply. Wills and King caught up and the trio rode into Depot Camp 65. Desperate now, they looked for the comforting glow of the campfire. There was none.

The three men stared in disbelief at the remains of the camp.

Undaunted, they reasoned that the base camp must have shifted further down the creek. Exhausted, they prepared to tramp the last few kilometres to find their companions.

It was Wills who saw the carving on the coolibah tree:

DIG

UNDER

3 FT NW

There was a date engraved on a low branch next to the message: April 21st 1861. King bent down to feel the ashes of the campfires. They were still warm. The men of the depot party were gone. They had left that day.

TWELVE

DIG

AS Burke, Wills and King stared at the word 'DIG' engraved on the tree, the terrible reality set in. Burke collapsed in the dirt. He couldn't move. Wills and King scratched away the earth beneath the tree. They found an old camel trunk with a bottle and a note inside:

> Depot, Cooper's Creek, 21 April 1861
>
> The depot party of the VEE leaves this camp today to return to the Darling. I intend to go SE from Camp LX, to get to our old track near Bulloo. Two of my companions and myself are quite well; the third—Patten—has been unable to walk for the last eighteen days, as his leg has been severely hurt when thrown by one of the horses. No person has been up here from the Darling. We have six camels and twelve horses in good working condition.
>
> William Brahe.

Underneath the note, there was flour, sugar, tea and some dried meat. Somehow King mustered the strength to prepare a meal. As they devoured porridge and sugar, a trickle of energy returned and the three men contemplated their predicament.

Their renewed clarity brought with it an even greater sense of anguish. They had been away 127 days. According to the message and the warm ashes of the fire, they had missed Brahe by eight or nine hours—about the same time they had lingered to bury Charley Gray.

Why hadn't Wright been up from the Darling? How far away was Brahe now? The obvious move was to catch up with him, but his note said that all the horses and camels were in good condition—how could they possibly hope to overtake a fresh party? Both Wills and King agreed that it was impossible to go any further that night.

Twenty-two kilometres to the south, William Brahe and his men were also settling down for the night. They were in a far worse state than their note suggested. It would be a slow journey to Menindee.

For Brahe, the decision to leave Depot Camp 65 was a release. For weeks he had fought a running battle with his conscience, scanning the horizon and reworking the possibilities in his mind. In the end, physical deterioration made the decision for him. Everyone except Dost Mohomet was starting to suffer from scurvy—without fresh food, decline and death were inevitable.

Burke had promised to be back in three months. Brahe had waited four months and one week. On 18 April 1861 he wrote:

> There is no probability of Mr Burke returning this way. Patten is in a deplorable state…and our provision will soon be reduced to a quantity insufficient to take us back to the Darling…Being also sure that I and McDonough would not much longer escape scurvy, I, after most seriously considering all the circumstances, made up my mind to start for the Darling on Sunday next, the 21st.

Brahe ordered William Patten to shoe the horses at once. The blacksmith collapsed soon afterwards. On the eve of their departure, Brahe burnt the packet of letters that Burke had entrusted to him before he left for the Gulf. It seemed like the final acknowledgment that Burke was never coming back.

On 20 April, Patten was unable to move at all. Brahe buried the camel chest full of supplies then took out his knife and carved a message in the old coolibah tree. Opposite the original camp number, he chiselled out the command 'DIG'. Then, on a lower bough, he inscribed his arrival and departure dates. The coolibah that had protected them for so many months was now a giant living message-stick. It was all that was left for Burke to return to.

At 10.30 a.m. on 21 April 1861, Brahe, McDonough, Patten and Dost Mahomet took one last look around Depot Camp 65. They mounted their horses and camels and headed for home.

Meanwhile, William Wright, was battling to keep his own party alive, let alone bring relief to anyone else. After leaving Menindee on 26 January 1861, it became clear that his outfit was hopelessly inadequate for the journey to Cooper Creek.

Wright's party consisted of Herman Beckler, Becker, Stone, Hodgkinson, Purcell, Cook, Smith, Dick and Belooch. They took with them thirteen horses and ten camels loaded with food. Dick, the Aboriginal guide, soon realised that tragedy was inevitable. On the first night, he slipped away into the darkness.

Wright was dismayed to find that the waterholes that had sustained Burke's party had shrunk to an undrinkable sludge. By the third day, Beckler found the horses were in a 'shocking condition'. They became so thirst-crazed that they burnt their lips trying to sift through the embers of the fire looking for water.

In early February the party followed Burke's track out through Mutawintji and towards Torowoto—but Wright's disorganisation hampered its progress. He was incapable of establishing a routine. The camels contributed to the disorder by bolting, bucking, kicking and biting during the day—then vanishing every night. Burke

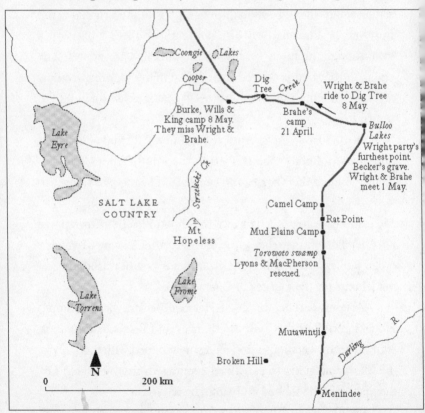

On 21 April, Burke, Wills and King returned to the depot camp; Brahe was just twenty-two kilometres away. They missed rescue a second time when Brahe and Wright rode to the Dig Tree on 8 May.

DIG

reached Torowoto in eleven days. Wright took seventeen. He arrived on 12 February 1861, just when Burke was about to turn south from Camp 119.

Wright's appearance at the waterholes was greeted with exuberant ceremony by the Wanjiwalku people, the tribe who had looked after Lyons and MacPherson. The next morning, two young men were persuaded to accompany the party as far as the next waterholes at Bulloo Lakes, 150 kilometres south of the Cooper. The guides indicated that the water along Burke's route had now dried up and pointed insistently in another direction, but Wright was reluctant to depart from the track. He needed to maximise his chances of meeting anyone heading south and was also terrified of getting lost. Without a surveyor, he could never be sure where he was or how far he had to go. The Aboriginal guides refused to follow Wright and returned to their tribes.

Beyond Torowoto the springy green pastures that Burke had found were now brittle yellow wastelands. Thirst dominated every hour. Beckler wrote:

> In these circumstances one treats this precious fluid in a quite different manner from when there is enough of it…I usually took a desert-spoon full of water every hour, some of which I usually poured back into the container. In the evening, just before going to bed, I drank about 4 ounces through a straw with great ecstasy.

A few kilometres further north, a new camp, Rat Point, was established on 19 February. It was crawling with vermin and flies. Despite this, Becker still completed seven fine paintings, including one of the long-haired rats that chewed at his feet as he tried to sleep.

With no obvious water ahead, the party remained at Rat Point for twenty days. Sickness was inevitable. Soon Wright, Smith, Belooch and Hodgkinson were suffering from 'dysentery'. The entire party was losing weight with alarming speed. Becker, Purcell and Stone were also showing signs of beri-beri, scurvy and barcoo rot. Stone had other problems. Unbeknown to anyone but Beckler, he had been suffering from advanced syphilis for some time. Now his legs swelled and pustules broke out over his body.

Wright decided to continue north on 12 March. Sensing more work, the camels escaped, forcing Beckler and Belooch to walk more than eighty kilometres to retrieve them. Soon after the party left Rat Point, Becker's horse died, and many of the men complained they were too 'knocked up' to travel any further. But stopping in the middle of the desert was not an option. They kept walking because they had to.

At the next camp Beckler administered what treatment he could. Ludwig Becker was housed with Purcell, who had descended into a delirious stupor. Both men had only the vaguest control over their bowels and often lay for hours in their soiled blankets. Yet Becker continued to paint. Propping up his bloated body on some old camel bags, he completed one more picture, fearing it would be his last. He described his state of mind as one of 'utter misery'.

Still Wright pressed on. On 26 March those men who could walk staggered towards Koorliatto Creek. The rest were propped on any animal still strong enough to carry them. Three days later, rain fell for the first time in weeks. It should have been a relief but it only seemed to chill the men and make them sicker.

The party arrived at Koorliatto on 30 March. Leaving Beckler behind in charge of the invalids, Wright set out again and found reasonable water up ahead at Bulloo Lakes. On 12 April, he sent Hodgkinson back to bring up the others, but Beckler refused—Becker and Purcell could not travel. The next day, after Hodgkinson had left to return to Bulloo, a group of Aborigines gathered and began a threatening vigil around the camp. Beckler tried to placate them but it was obvious that they resented the Europeans camping at their best waterholes. The doctor retreated to his tent and sat wondering if sickness or a spear would get him first.

Beckler endured Koorliatto for three weeks. In filth and squalor, he tended the invalids, refusing to move lest he should endanger their lives any further. On 21 April, when it was clear that his patients were not likely to improve, Beckler agreed to join Wright. Becker and Purcell survived the journey but only just. By the time they reached Bulloo, Purcell was hurling obscenities at anyone who approached him, Stone was defecating blood and 'had such pains in both his knee joints that he screamed aloud', Becker was fainting with every movement, Belooch was covered in sores, Hodgkinson had toothache and even Beckler had 'a catarrhal eye infection'. They didn't stand a chance of reaching the Cooper. In three months since leaving Menindee, they had covered 450 kilometres.

One hundred and fifty kilometres north, on the banks of the Cooper, Burke, Wills and King woke on 22 April 1861 in their abandoned depot. Daylight brought clearer recognition of their predicament. They were 600 kilometres from Menindee, cut off

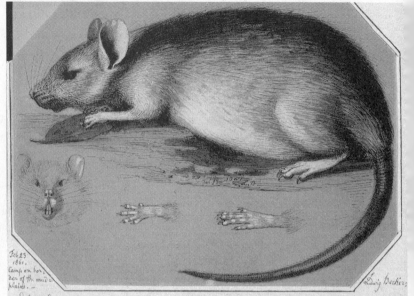

Feb 23
1861.
Camp on bor-
der of the mud-
plains ...

Color: dark ash-grey, the upper third of the hairs is pale brown & sandy colored, tufts of hairs, however remain-
ing black, giving the coat a dark patched appearance, underside dirty white. Nose, ear, feet & tail pale flesh color
these parts are covered with small white hairs, extending over the claws. The ringed tail covered with short black hair, 4 fingers
on fore-foot; thumb rudimentary, with a nail; Eyes black; 5 rows of bristles, the 3 first ones black, the lower ones white, are on upper-lip.

With hundreds of native rats scampering over him as he slept, Becker had no trouble obtaining specimens. The rodent plague indicates the expedition was travelling in a particularly fertile season.

by a lethal tract of waterless country with only two weakened camels.

Wills and King pleaded with Burke to follow their old track back down to the Darling River. If rescue came, they argued, it would arrive from that direction. But Burke wanted to try for Mount Hopeless, the South Australian police outpost 250 kilometres away, used by Augustus Gregory on his 1858 journey from the Cooper back to Adelaide. Burke was adamant that his party could retreat the same way, despite the fact that Gregory made the journey with eight men, forty horses and plenty of supplies. Even then Gregory had struggled. Burke's plan was madness but he was so insistent that Wills and King gave in.

An examination of the camel trunk revealed what Wills called 'ample supplies': flour, rice, oatmeal, sugar and dried meat.

The night before they left the depot, Burke wrote a sad, courageous note:

Cooper's Creek Camp 65
    The return party from Carpentaria, consisting of myself, Wills, and King (Gray dead), arrived here last night and found that the depot party had only started on the same day. We proceed on, to-morrow, slowly down the creek towards Adelaide by Mount Hopeless, and shall endeavour to follow Gregory's track; but we are very weak. The two camels are done up, and we shall not be able to travel faster than four or five miles a day. Gray died on the road from exhaustion, and fatigue. We have all suffered much from hunger. The provisions left here will, I think, restore our strength. We have discovered a practicable route to Carpentaria, the chief position of which lies in the 140° of East longitude. There is some good country between this and the Stony Desert. From thence to the tropics the land is dry and stony. Between the Carpentaria a considerable portion is rangy, but well watered and richly grassed. We reached the shores of Carpentaria on the 11th of February, 1861. Greatly disappointed at finding the party here gone.
Robert O'Hara Burke
April 22, 1861
P.S. The camels cannot travel, and we cannot walk, or we should follow the other party. We shall move slowly down the creek.

Next morning, John King reburied the trunk. He raked over the ground, and scattered the cache with horse dung so as not to arouse the suspicions of the local Aborigines. Then, he leaned the rake against a tree and with a broken bottle, cut a piece of leather from the door of the stockade to repair some equipment. When he finished, he placed the bottle on the edge of the stockade.

King asked if he should carve out a new message on the tree. 'No,' replied Burke, 'the word DIG serves our purpose as much as it served theirs.' To the casual observer, there was no sign that anyone had been there at all.

As Burke's party struck west for Mount Hopeless, Stone died at Wright's Bulloo camp. Purcell died the next morning.

As preparations were made for a burial service, Aboriginal tribes began harassing the camp. Using his limited knowledge of the local Aboriginal dialects, Wright ordered the warriors to leave the camp. Most retreated, but one young man came forward and attempted to communicate. Wright nicknamed him 'Mr Shirt'. He became an ambassador between the native and European camps, but the atmosphere of foreboding continued to grow. Mr Shirt told the men that his tribe were soon arriving to celebrate a feast and, Beckler writes, 'not to be too venturesome; neighbouring tribes were already coming to drive us away'.

Wright, determined not to show weakness, picked him up by the neck and threw him out of the camp, then ordered the men to stack up tree branches to provide crude fortifications. Only Ludwig Becker was oblivious to the danger. He grew weaker by the hour.

On 27 April, as Becker slipped into unconsciousness, the Aboriginal tribes returned with reinforcements. About one hundred men divided into two groups were moving along the creek. Beckler reached for his gun while Wright shouted, warning them not to come any closer. Mr Shirt gestured that there was nothing more he could do and the warriors rushed forward with their spears:

> At twenty paces Wright ordered us to fire. A few fell, several apparently from fright. Shirt fell right before us…He alone was severely wounded…He was a hero from head to toe…It was to our advantage that it was he, the leader, who alone fell, but we all felt sorry for this noble leader and representative of his tribe…he staggered down to the water and disappeared into the scrub.

No one knows whether Mr Shirt survived, but the sorrowful wails that drifted through that night air would seem to indicate that he did not.

Afterwards there was an uneasy calm. The men kept their revolvers at their side.

As Burke, Wills and King walked towards Mount Hopeless, Wills felt a new surge of optimism: 'We find the change of diet already making a great improvement in our spirits and strength. The weather is delightful, the days warm, but the nights are very chilly.' The Yandruwandha seemed pleased their visitors were on the move. As they followed the explorers offering gifts and laughing, Wills' harsh views began to soften:

> We had scarcely finished breakfast when our friends the blacks, from whom we obtained the fish, made their appearance with a few more, and seemed inclined to go with us and keep up the supply. We gave them some sugar, with which they were greatly pleased. They are by far the most well-behaved blacks we have seen on Cooper's Creek.

This constant bartering improved the explorers' diet, banishing their 'leg-tied feeling' and allowing such good progress during the next week that Wills began to lament the loss of his scientific instruments. But, on 28 April, as they walked by moonlight alongside the Cooper, one of the camels, Linda, became bogged in 'bottomless quicksand'. Exhausted by their efforts to free it, they stopped and camped. At dawn, they tried again, but it was no use. King shot the camel and the trio spent an unpleasant morning wading into the swamp and hacking off flesh from the carcass.

It was a bitter blow. Burke should have reassessed his plan as the situation changed and his resources diminished, but the three men set off once again towards Mount Hopeless, dragging their remaining camel behind them.

On 29 April 1861, two days after Mr Shirt had been shot, Wright and Beckler were woken in the small hours of the morning by horse bells to the north. Someone was approaching the camp. They ran outside. Could it be Burke returning?

As morning broke, a horseman appeared on the horizon. It was William Brahe. The two back-up parties had found one another in the middle of the desert.

There was a lot of catching up to do. Brahe was appalled to find Wright's party in such a wretched condition but he was also relieved that someone else was in charge. Wright was thankful to learn that Burke had disappeared northwards without waiting for more supplies. Since he had failed to return to the depot, Wright reasoned that his own failure to reach the Cooper was immaterial. There was no harm done.

Wright and Brahe debated what to do next. The combined party may have been larger but it also contained more invalids. According to Beckler, only 'one single tenuous thread' stopped them from turning back to the Darling. Ludwig Becker still clung to life, delirious and unable to recognise Brahe. A few hours later, he died alone in his tent. He was buried on the morning of 30 April.

With Becker dead, Burke presumed dead, and the rest of the men deteriorating fast, there seemed little else to do but retreat. But something continued to nag at Brahe's conscience. What if Burke had not gone to Queensland or perished in the desert? What if he had returned to the depot camp? Brahe suggested that he and Wright should make a dash back up to the Cooper, just to be sure. The two men saddled the best of the horses and set out for the Dig Tree at Depot Camp 65, 150 kilometres away.

As Brahe and Wright galloped north to the Cooper, Burke, Wills and King were still trudging towards Mount Hopeless. Their meagre supplies made them dependent on the hospitality of the local people. The tribesmen followed them like shadows, always ready with gifts of fish and nardoo, which the explorers swapped for their few remaining survival tools—fishhooks.

Four days after Linda's accident, Rajah began to show signs of being 'done up'. A few hours later he was trembling and sweating. He collapsed on 6 May. With the last of the camels gone, Burke should have realised that the journey to Mount Hopeless was futile. But the trio continued on, clutching a small bundle of supplies each. The Cooper splintered into hundreds of tiny rivulets and Wills despaired as every channel they tried to follow headed 'the wrong way'.

Wills explored the area but he was constantly confronted by 'high sand ridges, running nearly parallel with the one on which I was standing'. It was 'a dreary prospect offering me no encouragement to proceed'. Back at camp, the surveyor wrote, 'I suppose this will end in our having to live like the blacks for a few months.' One afternoon, he and Burke stumbled across several men catching fish:

> On our arrival at the camp, they led us to a spot to camp on, and soon afterwards brought a lot of fish and bread, which they call nardoo…In the evening, various members of the tribe came down with lumps of nardoo, and handfuls of fish until we were positively unable to eat any more.

On 8 May, Wills left Burke and King behind and set out once again to look for 'the main channel' of the Cooper. It was useless. On his way back he found that 'my friends the blacks' had made him a place to sleep in one of their gunyahs, and prepared a supper of fish, nardoo and 'a couple of nice fat rats'. As he lay down that night, exhausted, Wills finally acknowledged that the journey to Mount Hopeless was impossible. They were stranded. The last two and a half weeks had been a futile waste.

That same day, thirty or forty kilometres to the east, Brahe and Wright reached the Dig Tree. They attributed the mass of footprints and the remains of the campfires to the Aborigines. They didn't notice the broken bottle on the top of the stockade, the rake leaning against the tree or the piece of leather cut out of the stockade door. Everything looked exactly as they had left it. There were no new carvings on the tree. The two men felt relief. No one had been back. Their consciences were clear. Brahe and Wright stayed for just fifteen minutes before remounting and heading south to Bulloo.

THIRTEEN

THIS EXTRAORDINARY CONTINENT

WHEN Wills returned from his final reconnaissance mission on 10 May, he found Burke and King still up to their elbows in camel flesh. No one was ready to give up yet, but Wills was determined to convince Burke that they must abandon the idea of Mount Hopeless. He still found it hard to believe he was reduced to 'living with the blacks', but his interactions with the Yandruwandha had changed his opinions profoundly. Wills' reassessment was too little, too late. He, Burke and King tried to copy the Yandruwandha but living off the land was not easy. Wills had observed the Yandruwandha grind the nardoo seed into flour, but since he had never seen them collect it, Wills didn't realise it grew on the ground. Burke and King conducted a futile search of the nearby trees. Without fishhooks they couldn't fish and without nets they couldn't trap birds. Worst of all, the Yandruwandha, had moved off down the creek and disappeared.

Despite the overwhelming arguments for abandoning the journey to Mount Hopeless, Burke was still convinced escape lay that way. On 15 May 1861, he ordered his two men to bury the last of their belongings and set off once more down the Cooper, each man carrying just one blanket, some dried meat, a little flour and a billycan of water.

Wright and Brahe returned to Koorliatto Creek on 13 May. In retreat, the party looked more like an ambulance train than a relief expedition. William Patten wailed in agony on a makeshift stretcher on the side of a camel. Thomas McDonough spent most of the time unconscious and Belooch declared himself incapable of travelling. Even Beckler sank into despondency. The doctor was mystified. Despite anti-scurvy medicines and a broth of a local plant (mesembryanthemum), his patients continued to deteriorate. They still had nearly 400 kilometres to go to reach Menindee.

Burke, Wills and King found the creek difficult to follow but their spirits lifted on 17 May when King spotted nardoo on the ground, for, Wills wrote, 'we were in a position to support ourselves, even if we were destined to remain on the creek'.

Within a week, nardoo had become 'the staff of life'. Each morning they toiled for seeds to pound into flour. It was such an exhausting, time-consuming process it was almost impossible to travel any further. Wills does not record the exact date when Burke at last gave up the idea of reaching Mount Hopeless, but by 27 May, a month after leaving the Dig Tree, they had travelled approximately sixty-four kilometres from the depot camp to find the creek had shrivelled to dusty channels leading nowhere. Without water, they were forced to retreat.

Wills knew their chances of survival were diminishing and decided to return to the Dig Tree alone to deposit his journals, 'in case of accident'. On the way, he was reunited with his Aboriginal friends. They fed and sheltered him each evening. But his nights were wracked with agony. The new diet of nardoo and fish may have been plentiful but it didn't suit his digestion.

On 30 May, Wills arrived back at the Dig Tree. Seeing the deserted depot for the second time seemed to harden his attitude. Originally he hadn't blamed Brahe for leaving his post, even crediting him with leaving 'ample provisions to take us to the bounds of civilisation'. Now, he buried his journals with a note that revealed a growing sense of bitterness:

> We have been unable to leave the creek. Both camels are dead, and our provisions are exhausted. Mr Burke and King are down the lower part of the creek. I am about to return to them, when we shall probably not come up this way. We are trying to live the best way we can, like the blacks, but find it work. Our clothes are going to pieces fast. Send provisions and clothes as soon as possible.
>
> WJ Wills
>
> PS The depot party having left, contrary to instructions have put us in this fix. I have deposited some of my journals here for fear of accident.

Wills left the depot, unaware that Brahe and Wright had been there three weeks earlier. Now he was weakening. Too feeble to gather nardoo or hunt for game, he scavenged through the native camps, picking through the fishbones. One particular Aboriginal man, nicknamed Pitchery, assisted him, guiding Wills to a camp and feeding him. Wills believed that with the generosity of the local Aboriginal people, they stood some chance of surviving. But when he arrived back at Burke's camp on 6 June, a catastrophic scene awaited him.

Burke and King were sitting in front of a burnt-out gunyah. Their possessions lay in charred tatters around them and the native camp nearby was eerily silent. A young Yandruwandha man had tried to steal a scrap of oilcloth, and Burke had lost his temper and fired his revolver over the man's head. A few minutes later another warrior crept up behind King, laid a boomerang on his shoulder and, in sign language, threatened to kill him if he called out. It was a warning. The tribe could not understand Burke's animosity. Every day they brought gifts of food, yet when they wanted something in return, they were fired upon. That night the tribesmen tried yet again to restore relations by bringing gifts of fish and nets, but Burke knocked the nets out of their hands.

Later, Burke was cooking when a pan caught fire and set the gunyah alight. All the explorers' possessions were ruined. Burke had destroyed their last remaining lifelines. The Yandruwandha melted away into the bush. And Burke, Wills and King had no spare clothing, no bedding, no rations and no food supply except for the nardoo they could gather.

Wills left on the morning of 7 June to repair relations with the Yandruwandha. The tribe seemed to forgive the white men and even resumed their deliveries of food to Burke and King, but the atmosphere around the camp was uneasy. Two days later, the Yandruwandha indicated to Wills that they would be moving off up the creek. The explorers tried to follow but Wills found he 'could scarcely get along, although carrying the lightest swag'. With their rations exhausted, they took it in turns to look for nardoo, or stay at camp grinding and pounding the seeds.

The three explorers prepared their nardoo incorrectly. The Yandruwandha washed the ground seed and cooked it. The explorers consumed it unwashed and raw. The more they ate, the sicker they felt. By 20 June, Burke was so weak that he could walk only with great difficulty. Wills was worse, which left King to gather food for all three.

On 21 June, Wills acknowledged for the first time that death was a possibility:

> I feel much weaker than ever, and can scarcely crawl out of the mia-mia. Unless relief comes in some form or other, I cannot possibly last more than a fortnight. It is a great consolation, at least, in this position of ours to know that we have done all we could, and that our deaths will rather be the result of the mismanagement of others than any rash acts of our own.

While Burke, Wills and King clung to life on the Cooper, Wright's party was shuffling south, tormented by thirst, lost animals and the strain of caring for the dying. One by one the camels either expired or disappeared into the wilderness. William Patten died on 5 June. His departure was a relief for the rest of the men, who could now make better progress.

The party made it back to Menindee on 19 June. One observer thought the men showed 'symptoms of great suffering, particularly about the eyes'. The whole journey had been a waste of time. Four men had died and not a single box of supplies had been delivered to the Cooper.

Wright disbanded the remaining men and left town on the next steamer. Beckler and the other survivors hung about recovering their strength. It fell to William Brahe to deliver the news of Burke's disappearance and the expedition's disintegration. He set out at once for Melbourne.

As Brahe rode south on 22 June, the surviving explorers were camped by a waterhole the Yandruwandha named Tilka. Wills was confined to lying in an old gunyah and knew that he was fading fastest of all. On 26 June, he decided the only honourable thing to do was to sacrifice himself to save his companions. 'Without some change,' he wrote, 'I see little chance for any of us.' He suggested that Burke and King should follow the Aborigines up the creek to try and procure more food. This upset Burke. He insisted he could not leave his 'dear boy' behind, but Wills was adamant. He made a point of recording in his diary that the stronger men 'have both shown great hesitation and reluctance with regard to leaving me'.

Burke and King spent the day stockpiling nardoo for Wills. It was a harrowing time. In his notebook, Burke reveals his bitterness about their situation: 'I hope that we shall be done justice to. We have fulfilled our task, but we have been aban—. We have not been followed up as we expected, and the depot party abandoned their post.'

The next morning Wills refused to change his mind about being left alone. He maintained that his plan was designed to save the entire party, but he knew he would probably die while the others were away. As Burke and King prepared to leave, he wrote a last letter to his father:

My dear Father,
These are probably the last lines you will ever get from me. We are on the point of starvation, not so much from absolute want of food, but from the want of nutriment we can get...
We have had very good luck, and made a most successful trip to Carpentaria and back, to where we had every right to consider ourselves safe, having left a depot here consisting of four men, twelve horses, and six camels. They had provisions enough to have lasted them twelve months with

proper economy. We had every right to expect that we should have been immediately followed up from Menindie, by another party with additional provisions and every necessary for forming a permanent depot at Cooper's Creek. The party we left here had special instructions not to leave until our return, unless from absolute necessity. We left the creek nominally with three months' supply, but they were reckoned at little over the rate of half rations. We calculated on having to eat some of the camels…We got back here in four months and four days, and found the party had left the Creek the same day, and we were not in a fit state to follow them.

I find I must close this that it may be planted, but I will write some more, although it has not so good a chance of reaching you as this. You have great claim on the committee for their neglect. I leave you in sole charge of what is coming to me. The whole of my money I desire to leave to my sisters; other matters I will leave for the present. Adieu, my dear father. Love to Tom.

WJ Wills

I think to live about four or five days. My spirits are excellent. My religious beliefs are not in the least bit changed and I have not the least fear of their being so. My spirits are excellent.

Wills read the letter aloud to Burke and King to reassure them that he had written nothing detrimental about them. He handed over his papers and his pocket watch with instructions that they should be given to his father.

His last diary entry is attributed to 29 June but was probably written earlier:

…I am weaker than ever although I have a good appetite, and relish the nardoo much, but it seems to give us no nutriment, and the birds here are so shy as not to be got at. Even if we could get a good supply of fish, I doubt whether we could do much work on them and the nardoo alone. Nothing now but the greatest good luck can save any of us; and as for myself I may live four or five days if the weather continues warm.

Later that day Burke and King left Wills a billycan of water, nardoo and some wood for a fire. Wills watched them disappear around the bend in the river. He was alone in the middle of his 'extraordinary continent'. It is not known exactly when Wills died.

Burke and King set off up the creek. It soon became clear to King that his leader did not have the strength to go very far. On the second day King settled Burke down under a shady coolibah tree next to a waterhole known as Yidniminckanie and then shot a crow for supper. Burke managed to eat a little but he knew he had few hours left. He took out his notebook and wrote: 'King has behaved nobly. I hope that he will be properly cared for. He comes up the creek in accordance with my request.' Then he composed a last message to his sister Hessie, in which he revoked his will to Julia Mathews saying he had 'foolishly made over what I left behind to a young lady with whom I have only a slight acquaintance'. He wished to leave all he possessed to Hessie, apart from the 'few monies accruing to me in Melbourne' which he still wished to be given to Julia. He wrote:

King staid with me till the last. He has left me at my request, unburied, and with my pistol in my hand. Good-bye again, dearest Hessie, my heart is with you.

Burke handed his notebook and pocket watch to King with instructions that they should be delivered to Sir William Stawell.

He asked King for his pistol and then whispered: 'I hope you will remain with me until I am quite dead—it is a comfort to know that some one is by; but, when I am dead, it is my wish that you leave me unburied as I lie.'

They were Burke's last coherent words. King stayed with his leader throughout the night. By the morning the Irishman was speechless. At around eight o'clock, he fell into unconsciousness and died. He was still clutching his revolver in his right hand. Robert O'Hara Burke had died an honourable death. It was the end he had looked for all his life.

For several hours John King sat by Burke's body and wept. At last, he got up. With a last glance at his leader's corpse, now stiffening in the heat, John King set off along the creek to look for the Yandruwandha. 'I was very lonely,' he wrote, 'and at night usually slept in deserted wurleys belonging to the natives.' They were now his only hope.

FOURTEEN

THE SCARECROW

BY March 1861, nothing had been heard from Burke since he left Menindee five months earlier. In official circles, there was little concern. But not everyone was so convinced of Burke's safety. In March, William Wills' father started calling for a rescue party to be sent out. His cause was taken up by William Lockhart Morton, an amateur explorer who had been passed over for leadership of the expedition. Morton attacked the Royal Society remorselessly for its inactivity. In a letter to the *Argus*, he demanded to know: 'What has become of the expedition? Burke has by this time crossed the continent, or is lost. What has become of Wright? What is he doing?'

Whispers began to circulate that Julia Mathews had approached several newspaper editors to lobby for Burke's rescue. The *Argus* responded in April by joining the call for a relief party, adding that the public was losing confidence in the Royal Society. Georg Neumayer admitted it was 'rather strange' that no one had heard from Burke, but insisted that there was no need to send a rescue boat to the north coast.

As rumours and recriminations rumbled around Melbourne, Burke, Wills and King were drifting helplessly along the Cooper. It was June 1861 before the Royal Society took any action.

The Exploration Committee set up two sub-committees— the first to organise an overland party, the second to investigate sending a vessel to the north coast. For the overland mission, some factions favoured Neumayer as leader, others George Landells. The camel-trader was 'shunned by everyone', but anxious to claim the moral high ground by charging to Burke's rescue. The wrangling continued for several days and then produced a surprising result—a highly suitable candidate.

Alfred Howitt had spent several years surveying and prospecting for gold, without ever losing a man. He was experienced, calm, practical, determined and, to the committee's delight, he was also a Victorian and a gentleman. He was so well qualified that many people lamented the fact that he had not been around to lead the original expedition.

There was no time to lose. Howitt made meticulous preparations and in an astonishing feat of organisation, left Melbourne for Coopers Creek on 26 June 1861, a week after being appointed. He caught a train at Spencer Street station bound for Bendigo. From there he would take the coach to Swan Hill, where he would pick up horses and supplies.

Howitt took just three men: Edwin Welch, his surveyor, and two old hands from previous journeys, Alexander Aitken and William Vinning. They carried with them a satchel of letters for Burke, one from Julia Mathews:

> Dear Sir,
> It is with fear I now address you but I hope my fears will soon be allayed by hearing of you safe and sound…Hoping my dear Sir that you and all your party are safe, that you met with a pleasant journey & good feed which is a great thing in travelling, my dear sir I dare say you almost forget me but if you scrape your various reminiscences of the past, you will recollect the laughing joyous &c.

Cupid

PS My sincere regards to you; all the citizens in Melbourne join in love to you, bless your little heart. C.

Burke would never know that she had not forgotten him.

Three days after leaving Melbourne, Alfred Howitt stopped at an inn on the Loddon River. A few minutes later, a weatherbeaten young man entered the bar, looking for him. It was William Brahe.

He poured out the saga of Burke's dash north, and that Burke and his three companions were missing, presumed dead. Howitt was horrified and prepared to return to Melbourne.

A telegraph from Howitt forewarning the Royal Society reached John Macadam on Saturday 29 June. Reports of the expedition's demise swept through the city. The press speculated on the 'wildest rumours of death and disaster', predicting that Burke's entire party had been 'dissipated out of being, like dewdrops before the sun'. The Exploration Committee convened an emergency meeting on the Sunday, after which it insisted that all was not lost. Sir William Stawell declared publicly that Burke's disappearance could be 'accounted for on many grounds… His men might be knocked up with scurvy, or he might be in some place which it was not advisable to leave until the rainy season set in.'

In the light of this, it seemed sensible for Howitt to resume his rescue mission immediately, but as Wills lay dying on the Cooper matters were referred up and down through committees and sub-committees. Howitt sat helpless while the days slid past. It was 4 July before he could rejoin his men in Swan Hill.

Once Howitt was on his way, attention returned to the ocean-going rescue mission. Neumayer offered to sail to the Albert River at once. Politicians like William Stawell and Thomas Embling realised the voyage would also provide an opportunity to survey a site for a northern port, thus strengthening Victoria's claim to the land to the west of Queensland.

Aware of these motives, the Queensland government proposed a rescue mission lead by Frederick Walker, a bushman of renowned ruthlessness who had opened up huge areas of central Queensland for pastoralists. Neumayer was incensed at being sidelined and renewed his campaign to lead the rescue. The Victorian government was forced to intervene to break the deadlock. They chose Walker—a curious move given their territorial ambitions but they probably wanted to save money more than anything else.

The Exploration Committee then handed complete control of Walker's expedition to the Queensland government. Sir William Stawell was furious, realising that this was tantamount to giving 'a bunch of sheep farmers' a foothold in one of the most valuable portions of northern Australia. With this one careless gesture, Victoria threw away its chance to secure a northern port and change the political map of Australia forever.

Seizing the chance to consolidate its territory, Queensland appointed two parties. Walker would travel overland from Rockhampton towards the Gulf of Carpentaria. Pastoralist William Landsborough would sail to Albert River and travel south.

The South Australians announced that £1200 would be made available for a rescue mission from Adelaide. Nothing had been heard from John McDouall Stuart, since he had left the Flinders Ranges in January 1861, but the South Australians were confident he would be nearing the north coast by now. In Stuart's absence, they turned to another Scotsman to lead their rescue party. John McKinlay had twenty years' experience in the bush and an uncanny talent for self-preservation. His deputy was William Hodgkinson, the journalist and former member of Burke's party. McKinlay was to travel to the east of Lake Eyre up to Cooper Creek and beyond, if circumstances permitted. He left from Gawler to the north of Adelaide on 16 August 1861.

After months of apathy, there were now four rescue parties heading in Burke's direction from all points of the compass.

As Howitt rode to the Cooper in July 1861, John McDouall Stuart was six months into his second attempt to cross the continent. So far it had proved a difficult journey. North of the MacDonnell Ranges, he found himself battling 'very poor country indeed'.

By the middle of May, Stuart had passed his previous northernmost point near Attack Creek but found himself entangled in bullwaddie and lancewood scrub—nature's attempt to grow a barbed wire fence. It was vicious terrain. Men and animals were cut to ribbons as they tried to find a way through. Stuart rode for hours at a time, until his horse tottered with thirst and he could barely keep his seat. On 20 May, just as the Scotsman began to think his journey was a 'hopeless case', he stumbled across a series of waterholes that he christened Newcastle Waters.

Each night, Stuart retired to his tent with his pipe to work on his charts and sketches. Later, R. R. Knuckey, a government surveyor who used Stuart's maps, commented:

He was simply a marvel for horseback traverse. His map was so correct that we used simply to put a protractor and scale on it, get the bearings and distance and ride on with the same confidence as one would ride from Gawler to Adelaide. If we did not find the old JMDS tree we never thought Stuart was out but that we had made the mistake, and we always found it.

In the lush oasis of Newcastle Waters, with ducks boiling in the pot and fish baking on the coals, Stuart's men began to perk up. But the respite was short. Beyond the waterholes, the scrub closed in once again. In five months, Stuart had travelled only 250 kilometres further than on his last journey north and he was loath to give up now. He made at least ten desperate forays to the north but, by early July 1861, he knew he must turn for home.

On 5 July, a week after Burke's death, Stuart named a small watercourse Burke's Creek 'after my brother explorer'.

Fifteen hundred kilometres away from Stuart's party, on the banks of the Cooper, Robert O'Hara Burke's body lay rotting in the sun. As requested, John King had left it unburied and set off down the creek. His survival hinged on small things, a patch of nardoo, a piece of fish or a place to shelter on a cold night. For two days, as King lay in an abandoned gunyah recovering his strength, one thought kept surfacing through the despair. Was it possible that Wills had managed to cling to life? King took his rifle and shot two crows. Perhaps some fresh meat might revive Wills?

On 1 July, King walked back to Tilka waterhole. He arrived to find his friend:

> lying dead in his gunyah…the natives had been there and had taken away some of his clothes. I buried the corpse with sand,

and remained there some days but finding my supply of nardoo was running short…I tracked the natives who had been to the camp by their footprints in the sand.

Later that day, when King stumbled into the Yandruwandha camp, the Aborigines seemed pleased to see their 'old friend'. They cooked him some fish and pointed out a place in one of their own gunyahs for him to sleep. Several of the men indicated in sign language that they knew Wills was dead, but they kept asking where the third man was? When King signalled that he too was gone, several of the tribe began to cry. That night they brought extra food for the stricken survivor.

Most of the time the Yandruwandha kept King supplied with fish and nardoo but, every now and then, they gestured, frustrated, that he should return south. Some of the tribe grew so angry that they threatened to kill King, but others felt sorry for him. One woman named Carrawaw took particular care of him, building him a shelter and preparing his meals. Carrawaw became King's particular *ngumbu* or friend.

The Yandruwandha seemed anxious to know where Burke was, so King showed them:

> On seeing his remains, the whole party wept bitterly, and covered them with bushes. After this they were much kinder to me than before, and I always told them that the white men would be here before two moons; and in the evening when they came with nardoo and fish they used to talk about the 'white-fellows' coming, at the same time pointing to the moon.

But no one came. King continued to deteriorate physically and mentally. As the weeks passed, he followed his hosts up and down the creek, clinging to the hope of rescue.

Accompanied by William Brahe, Alfred Howitt collected his party from Swan Hill and marched straight to Menindee on 30 July 1861. The whole enterprise was a model of efficiency.

Menindee had changed even in the months since Burke had passed through. Speculators, prospectors and pastoralists in cabbage-tree hats now propped up the bar and Howitt realised that the tiny outpost was already 'an explorer's township'. While he gathered information from the bushmen, his men were plundering the stores Burke had left behind, amazed to find that he had thrown out so many essentials including lime juice, medicines and fishing gear.

Howitt reached the Cooper with incredible ease in twenty-five days, on 8 September. Five days later, his men found camel tracks. Soon he and Brahe were following the trail of discarded tins, scraps of oilskin and abandoned saddlebags that led them to Depot Camp 65 by the old coolibah tree. The word 'DIG' stared out at them from its trunk. Yet again the instruction was ignored.

Brahe and Howitt could see no signs of any recent disturbance so they assumed no one had been back to the tree. Howitt admitted that the mass of conflicting clues in the area 'puzzled me extremely, and led me into a hundred conjectures'. He left the depot, oblivious to the fact that all the answers lay just beneath his feet in an old camel trunk.

The rescue party continued downstream and set up camp at a place Howitt named Cullymurra, from the Aboriginal name Kaliumaru or 'wide lake'. On 15 September, Edwin Welch was out on a reconnaissance mission downstream from the depot camp when he realised he was being watched by a group of local Aborigines. As they scattered into the bush, his horse Piggy shied.

Welch regained his seat and saw that a scarecrow-like figure had remained in the clearing. As Welch rode closer, the man dropped to his knees and raised his hands skywards as if in prayer. Welch stared in astonishment. Beneath the grime was a white man. 'Who in the name of wonder are you?' Welch asked. 'I am King, sir,' the man replied. The name meant nothing to Welch who only knew the officers on Burke's expedition. 'King?' he repeated. 'Yes sir,' croaked the figure, 'the last man of the Exploring Expedition.' And with that the scarecrow broke down and wept. It was a year and twenty-five days since King had ridden out of Royal Park.

Howitt's Aboriginal guides, Sandy and Frank, ran back to Howitt's camp with the news: 'Find 'im whitefella; two fella dead boy and one fella live.' A few hours later King was carried back to Cullymurra—'a miserable object and hardly to be distinguished as a civilised being'. The Yandruwandha followed their charge back to Howitt's camp. They were overjoyed he had been reunited with his companions and stood around the camp 'with a most gratified and delighted expression'.

King was almost too weak to stand. Sunburnt, emaciated and clothed in the greasy vestiges of a pair of flannel trousers and a shirt, he wore a leather pouch around his neck. It contained Burke and Wills' pocket watches and their last letters home. He had clung to them for two and a half months since their deaths.

Howitt's physician Dr Wheeler prescribed his patient small meals of sugar and fat. King began to improve almost immediately but he found it difficult to tell his story without breaking down in tears. With a growing sense of horror, Howitt pieced together the jigsaw.

On 18 September, King felt strong enough to return to Wills' gunyah at Tilka waterhole. The sand was crisscrossed with dingo tracks and the corpse had been partially dismembered. Some grinding stones and a small supply of nardoo nearby indicated that Wills had died before his food supply had run out. Howitt's men dug a grave nearby and laid Wills to rest with a short Bible reading. The grisly ritual was repeated the next day with the discovery of Burke's body lying intact under the coolibah tree at Yidniminck-anie waterhole. He was clutching his rusting pistol in his right hand. It was loaded and cocked but had not been fired.

William Brahe dug Burke's grave, a grim task for a man who knew he would surely be blamed for his leader's death. Burke's body was wrapped in a Union Jack and buried while Howitt read from St John, Chapter 11.

Several men wept as shovelsful of red earth were thrown onto the flag. An inscription was carved into the tree nearby and the men returned in silence to their camp. Howitt said later: 'It is impossible to describe the feelings of sadness and awe that filled our minds as we gazed on the spectacle—the remains of brave Burke.'

John McDouall Stuart's party was still intact—but only just. When the Scotsman turned back on 12 July 1861, his men were weak, short of food and still faced a trek of nearly 2000 kilometres to reach Adelaide. Stuart knew he had pushed his resources to the limit:

> The men are failing, and showing the effects of short rations…
> I had no idea that the hills would terminate so soon in
> such extensive level country without water…they completely
> deceived me.

The return journey was torture. Rations were low, winter had set in and the desert sparkled with frost. Stuart was suffering more than most of his men and he became ever more reliant on his officers. The expedition reached Chambers' Moolooloo station on 7 September 1861. A week later, as Howitt was rescuing King on the banks of the Cooper, Stuart was on his way back to Adelaide.

He slipped back into the city to present his findings to the Chambers brothers and South Australia's governor, Sir Richard MacDonnell. He was surprised to find a gold medal waiting for him from the Royal Geographical Society. Stuart accepted it without ceremony. His mission to cross the continent was incomplete and, of course, he wanted to try again. Hiding the fact that his health was fragile, Stuart began to plan his next expedition. Money, men and horses were all procured with lightning speed.

Just over a month later, on 25 October 1861, Stuart left Adelaide but, as his cavalcade stopped at an inn, disaster struck. One of the horses panicked, reared, and struck Stuart on the back of the head. He lay on the ground unconscious, the flailing hooves crushing his right hand and breaking several bones. Stuart returned to the city for treatment but he never fully recovered the use of his hand.

On 24 September 1861, nine days after discovering King, Howitt was ready to leave Cooper Creek. A line of Aborigines waited outside the camp, summoned to receive rewards of tomahawks, knives, ropes, leather, sugar and flour. 'I think,' remarked Howitt, 'they understood that these were given to them for their kindness to the white men, and especially to King.'

Physically King continued to make good progress but his mind was still frail. The burials of Burke and Wills had disturbed him greatly. Often King stared into the distance, and when questioned he would burst into tears.

Carrawaw and several other of the Yandruwandha sobbed as King was lifted onto his horse and led away. On his way back to Menindee, Howitt passed through Burke's old depot camp once again. This time he took heed of the word carved into the trunk and found the buried journals, letters and maps. Over the next few days, Howitt read them with grim disbelief.

As the rescue party travelled south towards Menindee, King defended Brahe on several occasions. He also made numerous remarks about the 'neglect and mismanagement' of the expedition, which his companions interpreted as referring to the Exploration Committee.

Still apt to become hysterical, King suffered terribly on the journey home. Weak and self-absorbed, he was often strapped to his horse for hours on end. Progress was so slow that William Brahe rode on ahead. Someone had to break the news to the rest of the world.

FIFTEEN

AFTERMATH

WITHIN a few hours of the news reaching Melbourne, the whole colony was talking about the 'thrilling news'. The continent had been crossed. Burke and Wills were dead. There was one survivor on his way to the city. Melbourne was stunned. In Beechworth and Castlemaine, miners downed tools and gathered in the streets to hear that their former police chief had died a heroic death in the desert. By late evening the scandal had spread to Sydney and Adelaide. It sparked international interest with articles appearing in Britain, Ireland, Holland, Germany and America.

For several days Melbourne's newspapers printed special editions, and plans were under way for commemorative portraits, diaries and maps. There was nothing the public celebrated more than a dead hero. Sensing the popular mood, the *Argus* realised that Burke's death had given the colony something it had been searching for: a 'first hero'.

> The sufferings and death of the first white men who crossed the Australian continent will be household words in Australia…In years to come cities will arise where the explorers rested, and plenty will be found where the explorers perished. All honour then to the gallant four, of whom three died and one survives.

As more details emerged, the scale of the tragedy only increased. No one could believe that the expedition had fallen foul of so many coincidences and lost opportunities:

That they should have reached Cooper's Creek upon the day on which BRAHE deserted it—that the track which the latter mistook for those of the natives should have been those of the missing men—that BRAHE and WRIGHT should have walked over the ground where lay concealed the precious document which would have told of the whereabouts of BURKE and his companions—who in his wildest dreams could have supposed?

Burke was far more popular in death than he ever had been in life:

The story of his great achievement, if it is the saddest, is also one of the highest in the history of manhood. No fiction was ever half so romantic—no hero more valiant, bold or loyal.

Few dared suggest that the expedition was a failure. Burke had conquered a continent—and Victoria had proved itself to the world. Sir William Stawell lobbied Victoria's chief secretary John O'Shanassy to apply to the British government for the annexation of the territory Burke had discovered. For a time it seemed a real possibility that Australia might gain a new colony—a sort of 'Northern Victoria'—to be governed from Melbourne.

The news of Burke's demise was broken to Julia Mathews on 2 November. The next day, she went for a walk in the botanical gardens and lost the miniature portrait Burke had given her before he left. An advertisement appeared in the Melbourne papers offering £5 for its safe return. Some believed she was genuinely upset over the loss; others speculated that casting herself as the grief-stricken sweetheart of a dead explorer was a publicity masterstroke.

Preparations began for the reception of John King. He was now travelling by coach towards Melbourne. The further south he went, the more bewildered he became. By day, spectators lined the streets and cheered as his carriage went past; by night local dignitaries plied him with banquets. Everyone wanted to hear his story but, each time he rose to speak, he broke down in tears. Edwin Welch tried to help his companion but confessed, 'I could not torture him out of his passive, dead-and-alive manner.' So many women offered to 'look after him' that he was locked inside his bedroom at night 'for his own safety'.

By the time King reached Melbourne on 25 November, the mood was at fever pitch. The Exploration Committee had made detailed arrangements for King's return—he must not be allowed to say anything that might prove damaging to the committee—but they underestimated both the public feeling and the determination of a grief-stricken Dr Wills. When King arrived at North Melbourne station on his special train decked with garlands and bouquets, Dr Wills barged into his compartment and demanded an interview. With King cowering in the corner, Edwin Welch intervened and insisted that everyone was to remain on the train to meet the Exploration Committee at Spencer Street station. Dr Wills delivered 'a volley of abuse' and then burst into tears.

Meanwhile, John Macadam had arrived at Spencer Street to escort King to a reception at the Royal Society Hall. He soon found himself being crushed by several thousand well-wishers. The crowd surged forward, and into the train. No one knew what King looked like, so people charged through the carriages, accosting strangers and demanding to know if they were with the expedition. King hid behind Welch, who locked all the windows and doors to their compartment and swore at anyone who approached. John Macadam was lost in the crush.

Police reinforcements cleared a path to the carriage. Welch slung King over his shoulder, marched through the station and shoved him inside a cab. Dr Wills scrambled inside, insisting they make for Government House instead of the Royal Society Hall. While he and Welch argued, the cab sped away, pursued by more than thirty carriages and a hundred or so spectators.

King was bundled inside Government House to be reunited with his sister, Mrs Anne Bunting. Before he could leave, King had to meet the governor. He could barely stand to shake Sir Henry Barkly's hand.

The mob had descended on Government House and somehow had to be placated. The dazed explorer was led onto the balcony for a brief appearance, before slipping through a back entrance and away to his sister's house in St Kilda.

If anything, King's appearance inflamed public opinion. How could Victoria's favourite sons have been allowed to perish in the desert? Who was to blame? Burke was, for now, above criticism. The Royal Society wasn't. The *Argus* branded its members as:

> third-rate amateurs in science, of no special knowledge or experience in exploration, and having small natural capacity for the work…the plain, direct and obvious duty before the committee has been entirely and grossly neglected and to this cause mainly must be attributed the disaster.

Only the provincial newspapers dared to suggest that Burke might have been responsible for the expedition's high death toll. The *Bendigo Advertiser* published a series of letters criticising his leadership: 'Burke was not a fit man for such an expedition…his want of judgement, or his obstinacy rather than submit to his junior led to his death.' The *Geelong Advertiser* added that Wills was the real hero of the expedition.

Even Alfred Howitt pointed out: 'Without Wills, Burke would have been absolutely helpless.' These views infuriated Burke's supporters, who were even more outraged when Sir Henry Barkly announced that the expedition would be officially renamed 'The Burke and Wills Expedition'.

At first the transformation of Burke into a valiant martyr was promoted in official circles. Memorial dinners were held and endless toasts were drunk. But the strategy backfired on the Royal Society. The more Burke was praised, the more public fury mounted towards those responsible for 'sending him to his death'.

The newspapers began to ask if the explorers' remains were to be brought back to the city or left to rot in the desert. As usual the question provoked argument among the Royal Society. Should all the bodies be retrieved or just those of Burke and Wills? Would anyone care if 'lesser men' such as Ludwig Becker and Charley Gray were left in the wilderness?

Resolutions were made, overturned and redrafted until a decision was made on 11 November 1861. Alfred Howitt would be sent back up to the Cooper to recover the remains of Burke and Wills for a proper funeral back in Melbourne. The others would be left to lie in the desert forever.

Public unrest over the expedition came at a time of instability in the Victorian government. The new chief secretary Richard Heales was entrenched in a long-running battle with John O'Shanassy, who had supported the Victorian Exploring Expedition and provided it with government funds. Heales lost power in early November but one of Heales' last acts before he resigned was to order an official inquiry into the deaths of Burke and Wills.

It was the political equivalent of throwing a hand grenade into Melbourne high society. O'Shanassy had no choice but to accept the inquiry. He had been involved with Stawell in plotting a more political aim for the expedition but he didn't want this aspect of the project explored in public. There was still a hope that part of northern Australia might be annexed to Victoria. If it was proved that Victoria had established a credible presence in the area and that the expedition's failings were due to the mistakes of junior officers, advantage might still be made of Burke's crossing. But if it emerged that the colony was incapable of organising an overland party to travel to the north coast and back, then not only would Victoria look foolish, it would also find it difficult to stamp its claim.

O'Shanassy also had personal reasons for protecting the Royal Society. He held power with a slim majority and he was desperate to ensure allies such as Sir William Stawell were unscathed by the inquiry's findings. In the small world of Melbourne politics, a finding against the Royal Society would have disastrous implications for many of its most powerful figures. On 12 November 1861, when governor Sir Henry Barkly announced a 'full and independent' royal commission of inquiry, there was general public approval—but most people had no idea just how much was at stake.

The royal commission of inquiry into the deaths of Burke and Wills began on 22 November 1861. No mention was made of the other five men who had perished.

A distracted-looking and carefully coiffed John King poses for an official photograph in late 1861. A potentially explosive witness at the inquiry, he was
kept under close watch by the Royal Society.

In a typical conflict of interest, it was governor Sir Henry Barkly who appointed the board's five commissioners, despite the fact that he was also president of the Royal Society. The result could hardly be described as impartial. The chairman, Major-General Sir Thomas Pratt, was Barkly's father-in-law. Sir Francis Murphy was the speaker of the Legislative Assembly and a member of the Royal Society. James Sullivan and Matthew Hervey were also politicians with strong links to the Royal Society. The fifth member, Francis Sturt, was a police magistrate and the brother of Charles Sturt. He was the only man with any direct knowledge of exploration.

The inquiry sat for a total of twelve days. Of all the commissioners, only Sir Thomas Pratt attended all the sittings. The inquiry was as significant for what it omitted as for what it included. It did not ask how such an inappropriate leader had been selected or why an overloaded expedition had been dispatched at the wrong time of the year. Instead, the commission chose to concentrate on events after Menindee.

Since Burke and the Royal Society were untouchable, it was clear from the beginning that lesser players would have to take the blame. The obvious candidates were William Brahe and William Wright. Neither had influential connections; neither was allowed legal representation.

It fell to the secretary, John Macadam, to defend the actions of the Royal Society. It was not a difficult task. Macadam argued that Burke was given 'a wide discretion to do as he pleased'. His only specific order was to form a supply depot on Cooper Creek and establish a line of communication back to Melbourne. Since this command had been disobeyed, the committee could take no further responsibility for subsequent events. Macadam insisted that Burke had been expected to take the hired wagons as far as the Cooper, so the whole party could stay together. He didn't mention the repeated threats to Burke over escalating transport costs, or how the committee expected twenty-one tonnes of supplies to be transported with just a handful of horses and camels.

The inquiry moved on: why had the committee not acted sooner to confirm William Wright's appointment and send up funds so that he could mobilise his back-up party? Macadam maintained that the committee had no idea any action was required until Hodgkinson galloped into town at the end of December with the 'startling news' that Wright was still in Menindee. But what about Burke's dispatch from Torowoto, which referred to Wright's appointment? It arrived in Melbourne on 3 December. Why did the committee do nothing then? Macadam argued that it assumed Wright would have considered himself third-in-command because Burke had appointed him to the position. Further confirmation was unnecessary. It also believed Wright would start for the Cooper at once, so any further instructions would have been unlikely to reach him in time. Again, the explanations stood unchallenged. Macadam stepped down.

William Brahe was next on the stand. Almost all of his 279 questions were based on the assumption that he had recklessly abandoned his post. Alfred Howitt had already defended Brahe in public, even stating that, in similar circumstances, 'I feel that I could have left Mr Brahe in charge during my absence with perfect confidence.' This support was ignored as the commissioners began looking for explanations to five critical issues:

Burke's intentions when he left Cooper Creek?

Burke's instructions to Brahe before he left the depot?

Why Brahe chose to abandon his camp when he did?

Why Brahe returned to the Dig Tree with Wright?

Why neither Brahe nor Wright noticed that someone had been back and disturbed the cache?

The first question was the hardest to answer because Burke had so many conflicting plans that none of his men ever knew what was to happen next. No one from the Royal Society was prepared to admit that, right from the beginning, there was a plan to split the expedition in two once it reached the Cooper.

Brahe found himself in an impossible situation. On the stand, he did his best. He pointed out that since Burke failed to keep a diary or issue written instructions, he could not say for sure what his leader's exact intentions were—but his understanding was that Wright would be 'up directly' with more supplies. Brahe vehemently rejected the accusation that he had abandoned his post and his leader. He argued that he had no choice but to retreat if he was to save the lives of his three men. He truly believed that, once the three months were up, there was no chance that Burke would return.

But Brahe's arguments showed cracks under the pressure. If he was so sure Burke would not return to the depot, why did he bother to leave a cache of food, or the note stating his men and animals were in 'good condition'? Brahe asserted that the note and the supplies were not for Burke at all. They were for any rescue party that might come looking for them and the note was designed to prevent any unnecessary alarm. The explanation sounded hollow. Brahe stepped down, his credibility damaged.

The next morning, the commission produced its trump

card—Wills' last letter. It stated that Brahe had promised not to leave the depot except 'from absolute necessity'. These were the words of a man dying alone in the desert and Brahe was no match for their emotional force. Questioned about why he'd gone back to the Dig Tree with William Wright, the commission inquired, 'Had you a lingering suspicion he might be there?' 'Yes,' admitted Brahe, 'there was still a chance.'

The next witness was Thomas McDonough. He seemed determined to settle a couple of scores. Branding the relief party 'very disorganised', McDonough said Wright never had any intention of rescuing Burke because he believed the Irishman had 'rushed madly on depending only on surface water', and was either dead or lost in the desert. McDonough then turned on Hermann Beckler, suggesting that he had starved William Patten to death because he couldn't be bothered to prepare proper meals. Even the journalists were stunned. Having provided them with their headlines for the next day, McDonough retired.

Next on the stand was Menindee's postmaster, Edmund Wecker whose evidence backed up Wright's assertion that, as well as forwarding Burke's dispatches when he returned to Menindee on 8 November 1860, Wright also mailed a letter of his own asking the committee to confirm his appointment.

Wecker then embarrassed the Royal Society by describing the spate of bounced cheques that had resulted in credit being refused to the expedition. Wecker speculated that this might have been why Wright was so keen to receive his confirmation—otherwise he might never have been paid!

John Macadam stormed back to the witness stand. He was certain that no letter had ever been received from William Wright on 3 December and the only information the committee had to act upon was contained in Burke's Torowoto dispatch. The secretary defended the decision to send Trooper Lyons galloping after the main expedition. The commissioners did not ask him why reports of John McDouall Stuart's failure were reason enough to chase after Burke—yet the news that an unknown station manager was in charge of half the expedition was not worthy of any action. As Macadam completed his explanation, there was a mood of expectation in the hall. Everyone was anxious to move on to the next witness.

John King took the stand on 5 December. His opinions on the expedition seemed to have shifted now he was surrounded by the power of the Royal Society, and he began to insinuate that Brahe and Wright were to blame for the tragedy. Much of his evidence was so circumspect that it was suggested in the press that he had been coached before the inquiry started.

King's complete loyalty to Burke dominated his testimony. But as the questioning began, it became clear that not even King's blind allegiance was enough to disguise Burke's shortcomings.

Asked if he knew anything about Wright's engagement, King replied that he had 'heard a rumour that Wright had been appointed an officer', but he was 'never told formally'. The explorer declared again and again that he had never been privy to any detailed plans regarding the forward or back-up parties, then contradicted himself by stating that he was sure Burke never intended to head for Queensland and had always planned to return to the Cooper. Was it just coincidence that King was certain on the one point that was most damaging to William Brahe?

For several hours, he picked his way painfully through the story of the journey to the Gulf and then described the terrible disappointment of arriving back at the deserted depot. When asked about Brahe's actions, an undercurrent of recrimination infiltrated King's testimony.

Question: Suppose he [Burke] had been away five months he would still have expected to find them there?

King: Yes, we should still have expected to find the party there. Mr Burke said they should have remained at any risk.

King completed his evidence by recounting a conversation he had with his leader just before he died. 'King,' Burke allegedly said, 'this is nice treatment after fulfilling our task, to arrive where we left our companions and where we had every right to expect them.' This testimony completed an indelible image of Burke as the brave adventurer abandoned in his hour of greatest need. Someone must be punished.

Ferdinand Mueller was determined not to be that person. Despite playing a major role in the early organisation of the expedition, the botanist said he had been ill or travelling when most of the arrangements had been made. He faced just twenty-six questions and retired unscathed.

The day's final witness was William Wright who had arrived from Adelaide. He faced a hostile and sometimes savage inquisition. The commissioners' principal accusation was that his failure to rejoin the main party contributed directly to Burke's death. Wright defended himself with at least ten reasons why he hadn't left Menindee sooner:

> I did not have enough horses and camels to carry the stores.
> I did not have enough packsaddles.

I was waiting for confirmation of my appointment and my orders.

I did not have any financial means until my appointment was recognised.

I had to wait for the return of Trooper Lyons.

I was waiting for horses and camels to be sent down either with Brahe or Lyons.

I was worried I would not get paid.

I had to safeguard my family.

Once I got authorisation I had to buy and train the horses, jerk the meat and get the expedition together.

I was waiting for another surveyor and a back-up party to come up from the city.

Wright had made a solid start to his defence so the commissioners changed tack. What was Wright doing in Menindee while Burke was dying in the desert? Was he 'merely looking after the stock'? they inquired. 'Yes,' replied Wright, 'merely looking after the stock.' Sensing a small victory the commissioners adjourned for the day.

When the inquiry reconvened two days later, Sir William Stawell swept into the room and the tone of the proceedings altered. 'Possibly Your Honour would be kind enough to make a statement with regard to the general management of the expedition, the instructions that were issued, and the intentions of the committee,' Sir Francis Murphy asked.

Stawell's statements were fluent and consistent. He backed Macadam's view that Burke's only obligation was to form a depot at the Cooper. From then on he was free to choose both his route and his staff. 'The Exploration Committee,' said the chief justice, 'considered that Mr Burke had full authority to engage Mr Wright or anyone else who was necessary…this question of confirmation always seemed a mere afterthought.'

What about Becker and Beckler's repeated pleas for help from the Darling—why did the committee not respond to them? Wasn't it obvious, replied Stawell, they were dispatches 'merely enclosing some sketches', and since they were not from the expedition leader himself, they were not considered important enough for the committee to discuss.

But what about the bouncing cheques—didn't the committee take some responsibility for the expedition's financial troubles? Stawell conceded there were minor problems with 'some very trifling drafts' but he expressed surprise that anyone should be so petty as to worry about them.

The proceedings livened up again when George Landells appeared. Shunned by most of Melbourne as a deserter, Landells saw the inquiry as a way of setting the record straight. He stalked into the hearing and demanded the right to call witnesses of his own. This was, of course, out of the question. Landells was furious: 'I am to understand that justice is not to be had. The doors of the Royal Society have been shut against me.' And with that he flounced out of the hearing.

As the inquiry drew to a close, the pressure mounted on William Wright. The commissioners decided to return to the question of his delay in leaving Menindee, and recalled him. If Wright thought his long list of justifications had strengthened his case, he was wrong. The commissioners insisted that he provide a single reason. After cross-examination, he couldn't give them a single reason that they would accept. He stepped down, his head bowed and his reputation in tatters. The commissioners had won.

The last word went to Ferdinand Mueller. After studying Wills' diaries and maps, he had reached a startling conclusion. Burke's party hadn't reached the Albert River as they and everyone else believed. In fact they were one hundred kilometres to the east on the Flinders River. The mistake may have been due to Wills' failure to factor in the six-degree magnetic variation of his compass, but it is also possible that when one of the camels rolled over fully loaded, his chronometer may have been damaged. If so, then all his subsequent calculations of longitude would have been inaccurate.

Before the inquiry broke up, there was one more embarrassing matter to deal with. It was revealed that despite repeated requests from John King, the Exploration Committee had failed to pay his wages. According to the assistant secretary Robert Dickson, the reason for 'this scandalous negligence' was King's failure to apply for the money. The commissioners ordered him to pay up at once.

The inquiry delivered its findings in February 1862. The commissioners were aware that too little censure of the committee would cause a public outcry and too much would embarrass some of the most powerful men in Melbourne. Their report was a balancing act. It blamed Burke on four counts: for dividing the expedition at Menindee; for appointing Mr Wright without 'any previous personal knowledge of him'; for 'departing from Cooper's Creek…without having secured communication with the settled districts as he had been instructed to do'; and for not keeping a written journal or issuing formal instructions to his officers.

William Brahe was also reprimanded but less severely than expected. Leaving the depot was 'deserving of considerable censure' but the committee was of the opinion that 'a responsibility far beyond his expectations devolved upon him'. The Exploration Committee was criticised for 'overlooking the importance of the contents of Mr Burke's dispatch from Torowoto' and in 'not urging Mr Wright's departure from the Darling'. These were deemed 'errors of a serious nature'.

Wright bore the heaviest burden. His 'fatal inactivity and idling' was 'reprehensible in the highest degree'; he 'failed to give any satisfactory explanation of the cause of his delay', and this caused 'the whole of the disasters of the expedition, with the exception of the death of Gray'. This public scapegoating of William Wright and to a lesser extent William Brahe deflected most of the criticism away from the Exploration Committee.

Once the inquiry was over, William Wright retreated to Adelaide in disgrace. For many, he was the man who killed Burke.

The royal commission had managed to apportion blame relatively evenly between all the relevant parties, but if anything, the public's anger towards the Royal Society intensified. Most people dismissed the whole inquiry as a cynical exercise in political expediency.

There was one other issue the commission failed to deal with—the death of Charley Gray. Sympathy for Gray was growing. Newspapers began to wonder why Gray's remains were not being brought home from the desert. Rumours began to circulate that Gray's death was not accidental. King had admitted that Burke had struck the sailor in his hour of weakness. Had Burke hastened or even caused Gray's demise? Perhaps his body was being left in the desert in case it proved Burke's guilt? Was his death actually murder?

SIXTEEN

BONES

JOHN McKinlay, who had left Adelaide on 16 August to search for Burke and Wills, made a grim discovery on 21 October 1861. He was on his way to Cooper Creek when a group of local Aborigines guided him towards a waterhole they called Kadhibaerri, in the Coongie Lakes region.

The next day he found the body of a European in a crudely scratched-out grave on the shores of the lake about 110 kilometres north-west of the Dig Tree. Of course he knew nothing about the discovery of King a month earlier, and assumed that Aboriginal tribesmen had slaughtered Burke's entire party. His description of the body:

> Skull marked with slight sabre cuts, apparently two in number—one immediately over the left eye, the other on the right temple, inclining over right ear, more deep than the left; decayed teeth existed in both sides of the lower jaw and right of upper… body lies head south, feet north, lying on face, head severed from body.

McKinlay was mystified to find a second grave, 'evidently dug with a spade or shovel'. There was no body but closer examination revealed 'a piece of light blue tweed and fragments of paper, and small pieces of a Nautical Almanac…and an exploded Eley's cartridge'. Nearby lay a 'pint pot' and a 'tin canteen'.

When news of McKinlay's discoveries reached Melbourne, it provoked a furious debate. Had he discovered the body of Charley Gray? If he had, why did the skeleton bear scars around the head? Had Burke's thrashing been violent enough to cause Gray's death? The controversy was fuelled by Burke's detractors. According to William Lockhart Morton, King told Howitt's party that, after Gray was caught stealing, he had been 'knocked down, kicked, and so ill-used, that he [King] would have shot the leader, if he had had a pistol' and that 'poor Gray was never again allowed to eat his meals with the others'. An anonymous letter to the *Register* claimed King had also stated that 'Gray was thrashed unmercifully by Burke when near to death's door', and that he had died soon afterwards. King denied the reports. He maintained that Burke had never been cruel to his men:

> The fact is that poor Gray died on the 17th of April 1861, which was twenty-two days after he was chastised by Mr. Burke for pilfering from the little store on which we all depended. There is a discrepancy I admit between the record in Mr. Wills and my statement before the Royal Commissioners, but I may say in explanation, that I was present and Mr. Wills was not… on the last evening of his life Mr. Burke assisted Wills and I to make the poor fellow as comfortable as we could by covering him with our blankets, such as we had, to keep him warm, in the hope he might rally a little by morning. But he died in the night—died from sheer exhaustion. I wish that those who are now so cruelly attempting to blacken the name and the memory of Mr. Burke saw him on the morning of the next day weeping over the corpse, as only a brave and generous man could.

King's response went some way to exonerating Burke, but there was general suspicion that he was now just a mouthpiece for the Royal Society. Since the inquiry he had changed his views on many things.

In the years since the Burke and Wills expedition, there has been much speculation about whether McKinlay really did discover Gray or whether the corpse was a member of a different expedition (possibly even Leichhardt's party) or even just an unfortunate settler lost in the desert. The most important opinion available was that of John King. Given the body's scars, he had every reason to deny it was Gray's, in order to protect Burke from accusations of murder. Yet King was convinced that the corpse was Charley Gray from McKinlay's description. He described how he and Wills, 'tied the body up in a flannel shirt, trousers and a large piece of oilcloth' just as McKinlay found it and he even remembered the pint pot and the tin canteen discovered nearby.

But, if it was him, several intriguing questions remain.

Why were two graves discovered adjacent to one another? Why was Gray discovered in the shallow scratched-out hole and not in the other deeper grave, which had been dug with a shovel? Why was he laying face down, when the Christian burial position is face up? Why was his head severed and his flesh completely decomposed after only six months buried in a hot dry climate?

The mystery is only increased by the fact that several pages of both Wills' diary and Burke's pocketbook were removed before the official diaries were printed. We will never know if those pages contained more information about Gray's death.

Several expeditions have been mounted in recent years to find the remains of Charley Gray. While the location of the camp where he died has almost certainly been established, the body has never been found.

There is one final mystery. McKinlay noted that the Aboriginal man who led him to the corpse also had a recent wound on his knee:

> He showed how he had been shot, by pointing to my gun, and carried from the spot on another native's back. Besides the wound on his knee, there was another bullet-mark on his chest, reissuing between his shoulders, and four buckshot still protruding from the centre of his neck.

The man was wounded before McKinlay's party arrived, but who shot him? Had a skirmish taken place at the lake to which Burke, Wills and King never admitted?

John McDouall Stuart was convalescing from his hand injury in Adelaide when he heard of Burke's success in reaching the north coast and of his death. The news made him more determined than ever to cross the continent—like most South Australians, he believed that Adelaide could still grab the overland telegraph. Besides, Burke's route did not technically allow the Victorians to claim the £2000 prize for crossing the continent, since Burke's track was too far east of 'Stuart's country'.

Without waiting for his hand to heal, Stuart rejoined his men at Chambers' Moolooloo station. On 1 January 1862, flanked by his trusted lieutenants, Francis Thring and William Kekwick, he rode north once more, his right arm dangling by his side.

Stuart crossed through the MacDonnell Ranges and headed into the dreaded scrub country further north. The heat took its toll on Stuart's weakened constitution and on several occasions he was forced to send Thring and Kekwick ahead, because he was not well enough to leave camp himself. North of Newcastle Waters, the discovery of another chain of ponds, christened Daly Waters, lifted their spirits but the explorer admitted in his diary, 'I feel this heavy work much more than I did the journey of last year, and feel my capability of endurance giving way.'

Yet Stuart refused to turn back. His party entered the lush tropical forests of the Australian north, and reached the Roper River on 25 June 1862. Calculating that he had reached Augustus Gregory's east–west track, he knew the coast couldn't be too far away. But his health was failing fast.

The Roper led Stuart and his men into what is now Kakadu National Park. This new paradise was more difficult to cross than Stuart had anticipated. There was so much water that the rivers and wetlands barred their way. Day after day, Stuart forced himself back into the saddle. He even ate on his horse for fear that he might not be able to remount after his meal. Could he reach the north coast before his health collapsed completely?

In Melbourne, the royal commission was over, but throughout the latter half of 1862, Burke and Wills fever still gripped Victorian society.

Ignoring the summer heat, Alfred Howitt was already on his way north to retrieve the bodies of the fallen explorers. Yet again, Howitt achieved his goals with breathtaking ease. During one reconnaissance mission towards Mount Hopeless he confided, 'At Cooper's Creek I have left the main party building a fort, catching the finest fish in this part of the world and gardening.' Howitt returned a few weeks later to find pumpkins, melons and radishes thriving along the side of the creek. He settled down to a meal of horse steak and fresh vegetables—just a few kilometres away from where Burke and Wills had died from exhaustion and malnutrition.

After several weeks exploring the area, Howitt exhumed the bodies. Burke and Wills' skeletons had been mauled by dingoes. Wills' skull was missing (except for his lower jaw) and Burke had lost his hands and feet. Howitt collected all the bones he could find, wrapped each set in a Union Jack, and put them in boxes to be taken back to the city. He decided to travel back to Melbourne via Mount Hopeless and Adelaide, as Burke had tried to do eighteen months earlier. Yet again Howitt showed how easy the journey could be with the right supplies and preparation.

When he arrived the mood in Adelaide was sombre. The sight of the tiny black box containing Burke's bones was enough to silence even the most critical commentators. John McDouall Stuart was still out in the desert somewhere far to the north. Nothing had been heard from him for nearly a year.

Howitt set sail for Melbourne with his macabre cargo, arriving on Sunday, 20 December 1862. Standing on the docks waiting for the ship's arrival was a delegation from the Exploration Committee and a small elderly woman who addressed the men in a strong Galway accent. Ellen Dogherty had been Burke's nurse, his nanny and lifelong friend. Now in her seventies, she had decided to travel around the world to see 'Master Robert' one more time before she died. But instead of being reunited with her favourite son, she found herself surrounded by strangers watching his bones being unloaded in a tin box. At the Royal Society Hall Nurse Dogherty asked to be left alone with Burke's remains. She stayed for several hours, leaving members of the Exploration Committee shuffling uncomfortably outside as they listened to the old woman weeping.

Eleven days later, on New Year's Eve 1862, the Royal Society gathered for the formal ceremony of 'coffining' the bones of the two dead explorers. There was just one problem. The metal boxes were locked. John Macadam had the only key. It was late afternoon and he was nowhere to be found.

Embarrassment, impatience and anger rippled through the invited audience. Several other keys were tried without success. The members were about to force open the boxes when Macadam made an unsteady entrance into the hall. He explained that he had been so upset, he was 'overcome with a sudden indisposition', which prevented him attending earlier. The newspaper reporters had a less delicate explanation. Macadam was drunk.

Among much ostentatious sniffing and dabbing of eyes, the ceremony continued. But not everyone was as upset as Ellen Dogherty who had sobbed 'all the while'. Several members of the Royal Society slipped a couple of Burke's teeth and a few locks of hair into their pockets as souvenirs. (It later became quite common in certain circles to pass around Burke and Wills' body parts as a conversation piece at dinner parties.)

To everyone's relief, Dr Wills senior felt unable to attend. But in the absence of any other relatives no one had thought to provide a winding sheet to wrap up poor Wills. An assistant was dispatched and the explorer was eventually swathed in a piece of old calico.

For a period of fifteen days the public was invited to view the explorers' remains through special glass-topped coffins. Nurse Dogherty sat next to the coffin entertaining the crowds with bouts of loud and persistent wailing.

Veiled and escorted through in a private viewing, Julia

Mathews was one of the first to pay her respects. John King also visited the hall, but on seeing the remains of his dead companions he broke down and had to be removed. Up to 7000 mourners a day queued to see the remains. Those with enough influence were actually allowed to climb up beside the coffins and handle the bones. Pickpockets ran through the crowds and stalls sprang up outside the hall selling food, drink and commemorative handker- chiefs. More than 100,000 people filed past the bodies.

Now the whole of the colony prepared itself for the magnif- icent final act: Burke and Wills would be buried on 21 January 1863. It would be Victoria's first state funeral.

SEVENTEEN

ENDINGS

THE prospect of the funeral prompted renewed discussion about whether the expedition had been a success. Burke had crossed the continent first, but at a cost of seven European lives and one Aboriginal life. The official interpretation was that the explorers had achieved everything they set out to do. Sir Henry Barkly informed the British Colonial Office that the outcome was of 'the very highest importance, both to geographical science, and to the progress of civilisation in Australia' and Georg Neumayer declared that the expedition was 'the most brilliant achievement as yet on record in the annals of Australian exploration'.

But the question was thrown into sharp perspective by the exploits of the four expeditions sent to rescue Burke and Wills. With embarrassing ease, John McKinlay and his party of ten continued from Lake Massacre to Cooper Creek, and up as far as the Gulf. Here, he had hoped to meet up with the *Victoria*, but he arrived at the mouth of the Albert River to find the ship had departed. He then travelled south-east, crossing several crocodile-infested rivers to reach the Queensland coast, where he caught another ship back to Adelaide. The journey took him more than a year. McKinlay didn't lose a man.

William Landsborough had an eventful start to his journey. On 24 August 1861, he left Brisbane with eight men on the brig *Firefly*, only to be shipwrecked on the east coast of Cape York eleven days later. Everyone including the horses had to be swum ashore while the *Victoria* pulled the vessel free. Once it had been refloated, the stricken ship was towed as far as the Albert River. Landsborough struck south-west and discovered the Gregory River near the present-day town of Camooweal, before backtracking and heading south. Landsborough didn't lose a man.

Accompanied by eleven men, Frederick Walker set out on horseback from Rockhampton on 7 September 1861, and rode north-west to the Flinders River, where he found Burke's dismal final camp. He followed the old camel tracks south for a while, before running short of food, and turning south-east back to Rockhampton. Walker didn't lose a man.

The eight deaths on the Burke and Wills expedition now looked more unnecessary than ever. Including Howitt's journeys, the five rescue missions collectively covered more than 11,000 kilometres through harsh terrain, without a single loss of life. They opened up millions of hectares for pastoralists and miners and lifted the final folds of the 'shimmering veil' that had hidden Australia's central and north-eastern regions for so long.

It is ironic that the failure of Burke's expedition led to far greater geographical discoveries than its success ever would have done. The achievements of the rescue parties were outstanding but they worked against Victoria's interests. Throughout 1862, the colony petitioned the British government to annexe a new territory on the Gulf of Carpentaria. It was to be called Burke's Land. To strengthen the claim, Melbourne's Department of Lands ignored the evidence of Wills' diaries and produced several duplicitous 'official' expedition maps. These showed the explorers' return route well to the east of their outward journey. It was a deliberate attempt to make it seem as if they had covered more territory than they actually had. But the British had more important things to think about than the allocation of obscure corners of northern Australia, and in government circles the matter was ignored. Once again, it was private enterprise that dictated events in Australia's north.

Queensland's squatters soon realised that the country around the Gulf was not as hostile as they had feared. Hundreds poured in from the east coast to colonise the area. Thousands of kilometres away, the Victorians could only sit helpless as 'those wretched sheep farmers' overran one of the most promising agricultural areas in Australia. All thoughts of telegraph lines, railways and northern ports vanished in the desert haze.

Today the expedition stands in a very different light. The venture was a product of a wealthy and complacent colony. It belonged to a peculiarly British tradition—one that valued breeding above ability and experience. Given the history of British and early Australian exploration, it was not surprising that the Victorian Exploring Expedition was, at times, a fiasco. Once Burke had been chosen as leader, the die was cast. The enterprise was doomed before the first camel was ever saddled.

Burke was proof that, in exploration, bravery is rarely an alternative for experience. Burdened with ill-chosen staff and cumbersome supplies, Burke did not have the knowledge or the skills to reorganise the expedition. An explorer such as Stuart would never have set out with such an unsuitable outfit in the first place. As Alfred Howitt noted:

> It is evident to me that at no time was there the necessary means of conveying the 21 tonnes of equipment and stores from Menindie to Cooper's Creek. This could only have been

done if an organised train of packhorses or camels, or both, had been arranged…But such an organised service neither Burke nor anyone else in the party was, so far as I know, competent to arrange.

Burke's inexperience was aggravated by his impulsiveness. With good organisation his divisions of the expedition may have proved successful, but his flimsy management skills only confused his subordinates. To a great extent Burke's mistakes were due to his inability to think through the consequences of his actions. He compounded his errors by leaving his safety in the hands of men who had neither the authority nor the resources to ensure his instructions (whatever they happened to be that day) were carried out.

Burke's all-or-nothing attitude and his fascination with dying a heroic death made him a dangerous leader. His failure to establish any kind of foundation to his life gave him something in common with Stuart. Both men were lonely bachelors who had never found their place in society, and felt the need to escape in order to prove themselves. The critical difference was that, while Stuart risked all based on his extensive knowledge of the Australian landscape, Burke had no such experience to fall back on.

There is a perception in Australia that Burke and Wills were victims of a vast waterless desert. In reality it was too much water that contributed to their deaths. The constant rain on the way to Menindee delayed the expedition and the heavy monsoon weather up in the Gulf country took a heavy toll on the men and their animals. The explorers died next to one of the greatest permanent watercourses in central Australia. Thirst was never a serious problem.

As a feat of endurance, Burke and Wills' trek to the north coast and back was an amazing achievement. Trying to complete the journey as fast as possible was a major factor in Burke's downfall. In the end Burke became a victim of 'an excess of bravery'. Once in the desert he seemed to lose touch with reality, until he was oblivious to the disasters that loomed before him. Blinkered by the conventions of his era, Burke found it impossible to embrace the expressions of generosity shown by the Aboriginal people he encountered. His innate sense of superiority made it difficult for him to understand his new environment and so he starved to death in an area where indigenous people thrived.

Despite all his failings, there is still something romantic about Burke. He was a flamboyant, charismatic man who had never really lived up to his own self-image. He was a man motivated by emotion, and his passions had found their object in Julia Mathews. As William Howitt (Alfred's father) commented later, Burke was 'suffering under the irritation of disappointed love, which made him moody, fitful…restless at nights, hasty in the day and apparently undecided what course to pursue'.

Burke's fatal flaw was his talent for mistiming events. He missed the height of the gold rush in Victoria, the war in the Crimea and the riots in Buckland. His arrival at the Dig Tree just a few hours after Brahe had left seemed almost predestined.

Good planning would have overcome some of Burke's mistakes, but equally, just a tiny piece of good luck could also have saved him. Once events began to spiral out of control, the Burke and Wills saga became the expeditionary equivalent of the *Titanic*. No one believed that such a magnificent enterprise could end in such tragedy. Complacency was the final mistake. Overwhelmed by mismanagement and ineptitude on all sides, perhaps the most striking thing of the Burke and Wills expedition is not that it failed, but how close it came to success.

On 21 January 1863, the day of the funeral, the air grew warmer and the atmosphere heavy. All over Melbourne people prepared for the largest public event the city had ever seen. Visitors poured in from around the colony. The trains were packed and the pubs were full.

From early in the morning, people jostled for the best position along the procession route. Estimates put the crowd somewhere between seventy and one hundred thousand. Several hotels draped their facades with swathes of black crepe, stalls were set up selling Burke and Wills souvenirs, including commemorative pamphlets, medals, portraits, poems, even 'Burke Exploring Hats'.

Given the public hostility towards the Royal Society, it was feared that some members of the Exploration Committee would be too embarrassed to attend the funeral at all. A proposal was put forward that all members should walk together in the funeral procession as a sign of solidarity.

At 1 p.m., a hush fell over the crowd around the Royal Society Hall. People removed their hats, as the undertakers carried the explorers' coffins outside to the funeral carriages and the police began to clear a way forward. Led by the Castlemaine Rifle Volunteer Regiment and the Castlemaine Light Dragoons, the procession would make its way towards Parliament House before turning down Bourke Street, then into Elizabeth Street and out towards the Melbourne Cemetery.

As the coffins were slid into place, the police contingent came forward, raised their rifles to the sky and fired a volley of shots. The crowd fell silent once again. The funeral procession was about to start.

On the same day in Adelaide, crowds were also gathering around the city. Since dawn, workmen had been hammering decorations in place in the streets. Pavements were cleared of rubbish and water carts were towed up and down the main avenues to dampen down the dust. By noon, the streets were full and spectators were on the balconies and rooftops.

The clattering of hooves silenced the crowd and a procession appeared. At its head, a horseman carried a flag embroidered with the initials JMDS. Behind him was a small, wizened, hairy figure mounted precariously on a packhorse. John McDouall Stuart was coming home.

Stuart's successful journey across the continent was a triumph of determination and stamina. It had taken him more than a month to complete the last 300 kilometres through the Kakadu area to the north coast. Slowed by a maze of mangroves, mud and marshland, he had finally approached the ocean on 24 July 1862. Even then, he kept his suspicions of success to himself:

> At eight and a half miles coming on a plain I could hear the wash of the waters and seeing a dense heavy bushy scrub on the other side of the plain, I knew it at once to be the bounding of the sea…Thring and I rode forward a yard or two and were on the beach delighted to see the broad expanse of salt water. I immediately dismounted, walked into the water, or rather dipped my feet into the Indian Ocean as I promised Sir Richard MacDonnell I would do if I got the chance, and not only did I do this but I washed my hands and face in it as well.

Thring got so excited at first sight of it that he could not restrain himself but called out, the sea, the sea, the sea, which so took the rest of the party by surprise that they seemed quite bewildered, and he had to repeat the words two or three times before they could understand him.

Stuart had emerged on a headland now named Point Stuart. After a ceremony to raise the Union Jack and toast the British empire, Stuart's men approached their leader to ask for an extra cup of tea by means of celebration. Stuart refused.

One of his men said later that although their leader was 'in their black books for a few days', they realised that Stuart denied the request because he thought it unlikely he would survive the return journey. He wanted to be sure there would be enough rations for the rest of his party to get home. From now on speed was essential. For the first few days Stuart was strong enough to lead the march south but scurvy was beginning to take its toll once more and his eyesight was now so afflicted that he could not see at all after dark.

In early October 1862, as the party retraced their steps past Attack Creek, Stuart was finding it hard to sustain the necessary twelve-hour days in the saddle:

What a miserable life mine is now. I get no rest night or day from this terrible gnawing pain, the nights are too long and the days are too long, and I am so weak that I am hardly able to move about the camp.

Stuart now had to be lifted on and off his horse. He could barely walk and strips of rotting flesh inside his mouth made it difficult for him to eat. By 18 October, the situation became critical:

While taking a drink of water, I was seized with a violent fit of vomiting blood and mucus, which lasted about five minutes and has nearly killed me…I have kept King and Nash with me in case of my dying during the night, as it would be lonely for one young man to be there by himself. Wind south-east.

The next morning Stuart was unable to stand. His men constructed a stretcher, which they tied between the two quietest horses, and it was in this giant sling that the explorer was carried south. For the last few days of the journey home, Stuart's men were convinced their leader was dying. He lay semiconscious in his stretcher and was only just lucid when the emaciated party arrived back at the outpost of Mount Margaret Station on 27 November

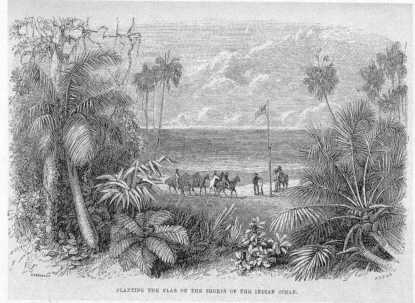

PLANTING THE FLAG ON THE SHORES OF THE INDIAN OCEAN.

Stuart celebrated his crossing by raising a Union Jack lovingly embroidered with his name by James Chambers' daughter Mary. Stuart named the area Chambers Bay.

Shops and offices closed as around three-quarters of Melbourne's population turned out to mourn their heroes.

1862. It had taken three attempts but John McDouall Stuart had at last achieved his dream. He had crossed Australia from coast to coast.

The party recuperated for several weeks in the Flinders Ranges before setting off for their reception in Adelaide.

Stuart himself was still weak, prone to violent stomach pains and choking fits, but he managed to ride unaided through the streets of Adelaide. As he passed the crowd cheered and waved their flags. Their hero had returned. 'The poor horses,' wrote one observer, 'they look so tired.'

In Melbourne, the procession was moving forward. Around the funeral car marched the pallbearers: John King (still pale and prone to fits of sobbing), Sir William Stawell, Ambrose Kyte, Frederick Standish (Burke's old boss), Alfred Howitt, Ferdinand Mueller and Dr Richard Eades.

Six mourning carriages followed. The entire cavalcade was so long it occupied several streets at once and it took more than two and a half hours to march the five kilometres to the cemetery. This was the most glorious spectacle Victoria had ever seen, even more glorious than the party which had marched out of Royal Park nearly two and a half years earlier.

At the cemetery the bodies of Robert O'Hara Burke and William John Wills were lowered into the grave and laid side by side. A police guard fired three volleys of shots as a mark of respect.

In Adelaide, John McDouall Stuart dismounted and stepped awkwardly onto the stage. As he accepted the keys to the city of Adelaide, it seemed as if the whole of South Australia was cheering his name. A few streets away in the city surveyor's office, his maps were already being scrutinised by engineers as they plotted the route for the new overland telegraph line.

In both cities, the sultry northerly breeze was blowing down from the desert once more.

EPILOGUE

IF Victoria had capitalised on Burke's journey and annexed a new colony in the Gulf country, the map of Australia could have been changed forever. As it was, the Victorians gained nothing, politically or territorially, from the Burke and Wills expedition. The unclaimed land between the 138° and 141° meridians was incorporated into Queensland in 1862, and after Stuart's journeys South Australia extended its northern boundary to take in what is now the Northern Territory. For many years Adelaide controlled central Australia from coast to coast.

South Australia won the fight for the overland telegraph line and the British–Australia Telegraph Company began construction in 1870. An underwater cable was taken from Java and landed on the northern Australian coast near present-day Darwin. It followed Stuart's original route almost all the way.

The first telegram from London to Adelaide was sent on 22 August 1872. Later, a road from Adelaide to Darwin via Alice Springs was built alongside the telegraph line. It is now known as the Stuart Highway.

John McDouall Stuart never recovered from his last exped-ition. He received the £2000 reward for crossing the continent, which gave him an annual pension of £162 a year, barely enough to live on. His only other rewards were a gold watch and a Patrons Medal from the Royal Geographical Society. He sailed to London in 1865 where he lived in relative poverty, cared for by his widowed sister until his death on 5 June 1866, aged fifty-one. Former members of his expeditions never forgot their leader. They gathered once a year, until their deaths, to drink his health with a bottle of the finest malt whisky.

In Melbourne, the Exploration Committee continued to meet for several years after the funeral, tying up various loose ends and even suggesting another search for Ludwig Leichhardt. A final set of accounts for the Burke and Wills expedition put the cost at £57,840, more than five times the original budget. The Royal Society exists today and meets in the same building in La Trobe Street.

Tributes to Burke and Wills continued for many years. Burke was awarded a gold medal from the Royal Geographical Society in London but since only one could be made to any expedition, Wills missed out and King was sent a gold watch instead. Dick the Aboriginal tracker was awarded a brass medal and £5 for saving Trooper Lyons and Alexander MacPherson.

A thirty-four-tonne monolith was placed over Burke and Wills' Melbourne graves in 1864 and a giant bronze statue of the explorers was erected on the corner of Collins and Russell streets in 1865. It has now been moved to Swanston Street. Major memorials were erected in Castlemaine and Beechworth and the expedition is remembered with countless plaques and memorial cairns throughout Victoria and Queensland.

The Victorian government awarded pensions of £60 a year to Nurse Dogherty, £120 a year to Wills' mother and payments of £500 to each of his sisters. When Dr Wills senior decided to return to England, the committee couldn't wait to hand over the £125 to cover his fare. Dost Mohomet, disabled by a rogue camel in Menindee, was given £200 and lived in the tiny outpost for the rest of his life. Charley Gray's family received nothing.

Hermann Beckler's career as a doctor and explorer in Australia ended in failure. He returned to Germany in 1862 in a fit of pique, when the Exploration Committee declined to give him a reference on the grounds that the royal commission was still investigating the expedition. He continued to practise medicine until he died in 1914.

Ludwig Becker was remembered with affection by sections of the German community in Melbourne, but his contribution to the art and literature of Australian exploration has never been fully recognised. The beautiful sketches he made during his time with the expedition are now stored in the State Library of Victoria.

Soon after Burke and Wills' funeral, John Macadam sued the *Argus* over claims that he was drunk during the coffining of Burke's bones. He continued in his numerous public positions until his death from pleurisy in 1865. He was thirty-eight.

After Alfred Howitt's successful journeys to the Cooper, he was appointed a police magistrate and goldfields warden for the Gippsland area, positions he held for the next twenty-five years. He became interested in geology and anthropology, leading many prospecting parties through eastern Victoria and writing several books on Australia's Aboriginal people. William Brahe continued to defend himself for many years after he was pilloried at the royal commission. Backed up by Howitt and the German community in Melbourne, his character underwent a significant public rehabilitation. He worked for a time in Fiji and as a pastoralist in Queensland. Brahe died in Melbourne in 1912. Wills' patron Georg Neumayer continued his eccentric scientific career, focusing his efforts on establishing the earth's magnetic fields.

William Wright faded into relative obscurity as a farmer on the Darling River. In 1863, he was one of the first to mount a search party for a missing lands commissioner, but he never recovered his good name. History has judged him harshly with many books and newspaper articles branding him the principal villain in the Burke and Wills disaster.

After Burke's funeral, Julia Mathews gave several memorial performances for the dead explorers. In 1864 she married her manager William Mumford, a drunk who beat her and used her income to support his debauched lifestyle. The couple had three children. Julia sailed to England in 1867 and became the first Australian-trained singer to perform at Covent Garden. She filed for separation from her husband in 1870 and went on to tour Europe and America. Later she became a devout Catholic. She died in St Louis, Missouri, of 'malarial disease'. She was thirty-four.

There were calls after the expedition for more appreciation to be shown to the Aboriginal people who had cared for the stricken explorers and saved King's life. In what they supposed to be a generous gesture, the South Australian government 'gave' the Aborigines 670 square kilometres of land around Cooper Creek in 1863. The gift was soon exposed as a ruse to start a Lutheran Mission and promote the gospel amongst the indigenous population. The project collapsed and native rights to the land were revoked in 1869. By that time the cattlemen had arrived and the dismantling of the traditional cultures was under way. Many indigenous people were moved away to Christian missions and their descendants are now scattered throughout New South Wales and Queensland.

As European settlement spread, camels became instrumental in opening up central Australia. They were imported from India and the Middle East and were used to carry materials for the construction of telegraph lines, railways and roads. Over the years, many escaped into the wild and there are now up to half a million roaming Australia's interior.

Today there is little physical evidence to mark Burke and Wills' transcontinental crossing. Their exact route has been much discussed over the years and confused by inaccuracies in Wills' maps, misreadings of his diaries, fake 'Burke and Wills trees' and numerous local myths. Some sections of the Burke and Wills route run through private land or terrain that is inaccessible, even by four-wheel-drive, but it is possible to follow portions of the journey on public roads and tracks, and to see some of the genuine campsites and carved trees. Burke and Wills' original graves on the Cooper are marked with cairns, as is the waterhole where King was found. They can be reached from the small outpost of Innamincka in South Australia. Howitt's depot at Cullymurra waterhole remains one of the prettiest places to camp on Cooper Creek.

Some of the desert country that the explorers encountered is still much as they would have seen it, but the introduction of cattle into more fertile regions has caused extensive soil erosion and a subsequent loss of woodland habitat. Rabbits have destroyed large tracts of land. Areas such as the Simpson Desert and the far north-western corner of New South Wales have been designated as national parks, while other parts are used for farming. Oil and gas have been discovered in the Cooper basin and sections of the desert now echo with the thump of seismic exploration.

The Dig Tree stands on the Nappa Merrie cattle station, just inside the Queensland border. The old coolibah has survived droughts, floods and termite infestations for an estimated 350 years. Since William Brahe carved his famous inscription, it has been the subject of much speculation and argument. So many versions of the message have been included in historical accounts of the expedition that there is considerable confusion about exactly what was engraved into the tree. But, by examining early photographs and studying the testimonies of William Brahe, John King and Alfred Howitt, it is possible to decipher the original message.

The most common interpretation of the original inscription is that it read 'DIG 3FT NW', with an arrow underneath pointing from left to right. But examination of photographs taken in the 1920s and 1930s clearly shows the word 'under' carved into the trunk: DIG UNDER 3FT NW.

John King, the only survivor of Burke's final party, returned to live with his sister in St Kilda. He was 'disabled for life—thoroughly shattered in body and weakened in mind, by his great sufferings' and never recovered 'a semblance of health or spirits'. He married his cousin Mary in 1872, but died a year later aged thirty-four from 'pulmonary consumption', a disease he had probably carried with him throughout the expedition. In 1863, the government granted him a pension of just £180 a year. It was not extended to his wife after his death.

Descendants of the Yandruwandha still remember the stories of their ancestors caring for a solitary white man stranded on the Cooper.

John King's descendants, now based in Ireland and New Zealand, have long known of an enduring connection between the explorer and his saviours. Their beliefs coincide with a story now acknowledged by senior members of the Yandruwandha. In 1867 a drover named James Arnold, also known as 'Narran Jim', was riding through the Cooper area. He came across a little half-caste girl around five or six years old who was living with the Aboriginal people. She was nicknamed 'Yellow Alice' and 'Miss King'. The Yandruwandha alive today believe she was John King's daughter.

TIMELINE

1860

2 March	John McDouall Stuart sets out to cross Australia
20 June	Robert O'Hara Burke chosen as leader of expedition
26 June	Stuart's expedition party is forced to retreat
20 August	Victorian Exploring Expedition departs from Royal Park
12 September	Depart Swan Hill for the desert, with new members including Charley Gray
14 October	Burke arrives at Menindee
16 October	George Landells resigns
17 October	Burke hires William Wright
19 October	Burke splits his party leaving half at Menindee
29 October	Burke's party reaches Torowoto Swamp. Wright promoted to third-in-charge and told to return to Menindee to recover stores and meet them at Cooper Creek
11 November	Burke and Wills reach Cooper Creek.
3 December	Burke's letters asking for funds and approval of Wright's position arrive in Melbourne. Committee fails to respond
16 December	Burke departs from Cooper Creek with Wills, Gray, and King
22 December	Hodgkinson leaves Menindee to deliver Wright's request for authorisation and funds to Melbourne

1861

9 January	Confirmation of Wright's position and £400 for supplies received
11 January	Stuart departs to attempt to cross the country again
26 January	Wright sets out from Menindeee
30 January	Burke reaches Gregory's track

13 February	Burke, Wills, King and Gray begin return journey
17 April	Gray dies
21 April	10:30 am Brahe's party leaves Cooper Creek
21 April	Dusk Burke and Wills arrive at deserted Cooper Creek
23 April	Burke's team head for Mt Hopeless
29 April	Paths of the two back-up parties converge, Becker dies
30 April	Brahe and Wright depart to revisit Dig Tree
13 May	Wright and Brahe return to Koorliatto Creek, back-up parties begin retreat
27 May	Burke, Wills and King abandon attempt to reach Mt Hopeless
30 May	Wills returns to Dig Tree to bury journals
6 June	Wills arrives back at Burke's camp
19 June	Back-up teams reach Menindee
26 June	Wills sacrifices self for party—tells Burke and King to follow Aborigines up the creek and get food
26 June	Rescue team led by Alfred Howitt departs Melbourne to find Burke and Wills
29 June	Burke dies, King left to travel on alone
29 June	Brahe meets Howitt and delivers news of expeditions, Howitt telegraphs it back to Melbourne
7 September	John McDouall Stuart returns to Adelaide after another failed attempt
8 September	Howitt arrives at Cooper Creek
15 September	Edwin Welch discovers King
21 October	John McKinlay discovers what is believed to be Gray's body
12 November	Governor Sir Henry Barkly announces full independent royal commission inquiry
25 November	King reaches Melbourne

1862

24 July   John McDouall Stuart reaches the ocean

1863

21 January   Funeral for Burke and Wills
21 January   John McDouall Stuart returns to Adelaide triumphant

SELECT BIBLIOGRAPHY

THE BURKE AND WILLS EXPEDITION

Bergin, Tom, In the Steps of Burke and Wills, ABC/Griffin Press Ltd, Sydney, 1981.

Bonyhady, Tim, Burke and Wills: From Melbourne to Myth, David Ell Press, Sydney, 1991.

Clune, Frank, Dig: The Burke and Wills Saga, Angus & Robertson, Sydney, 1991 (first pub. 1937).

Colwell, Max, The Journey of Burke and Wills, Paul Hamlyn, Sydney, 1971.

Corke, David, Partners in Disaster: The Story of Burke and Wills, Nelson, Sydney, 1985.

Jackson, Andrew, Robert O'Hara Burke and the Australian Exploring Expedition of 1860, Smith Elder, London, 1862.

Moorehead, Alan, Cooper's Creek, Hamish Hamilton, London, 1963.

White, John, The Stockade and the Tree, Footprint Press, Melbourne, 1992.

EXPEDITION DIARIES

Beckler, Hermann, A Journey to Cooper's Creek, Stephen Jeffries and Michael Kertesz (trans. and eds), Melbourne University Press and State Library of Victoria, Melbourne, 1993.

Davis, John, Tracks of McKinlay and Party across Australia, Sampson, Low, London, 1863.

The Explorers, Tim Flannery (ed.), Text Publishing, Melbourne, 1998.

Flinders, Matthew, Terra Australis, Tim Flannery (ed.), Text Publishing, Melbourne, 2000.

Gregory, Augustus C., and Gregory, Francis T., Journals of
   Australian Explorations, J. C. Beal, Brisbane, 1884.

Landsborough, William, Journal of Landsborough's Expedition from
   Carpentaria in Search of Burke and Wills, Libraries Board of
   South Australia, Adelaide, 1963.

Leichhardt, Ludwig, Journal of an Overland Expedition in Australia
   from Moreton Bay to Port Essington, T & W Boone, London,
   1847.

McKinlay, John, Journal of Exploration in the Interior of Australia,
   Libraries Board of South Australia, Adelaide, 1962.

Mitchell, Thomas Livingstone, Three Expeditions into the Interior
   of Eastern Australia, with Descriptions of the Recently Explored
   Region of Australia Felix, and the Present Colony of New South
   Wales, vols I & II, T & W Boone, London, 1838.

Stuart, John McDouall, Explorations in Australia: The Journals of
   John McDouall Stuart, during the Years 1858, 1859, 1860, 1861
   and 1862; When He Fixed the Centre of the Continent and
   Successfully Crossed It from Sea to Sea, William Hardman (ed.),
   2nd edn, Saunders, Otley & Co., London, 1865.

Stuart, John McDouall, Exploration of the Interior: Diary of J. M.
   Stuart from March 2 to September 3, 1860, S. A. Government
   Printer, Adelaide, 1860.

Sturt, Charles, Journal of the Central Australian Expedition,
   J. Waterhouse (ed.), Caliban Books, London, 1984.

Sturt, Charles, Narrative of an Expedition into Central Australia:
   Performed under the Authority of Her Majesty's Government
   during the Years 1844, 5 and 6; Together with a Notice of the
   Province of South Australia in 1847, vols I & II, T & W Boone,
   London, 1849.

Sturt, Charles, Two Expeditions into the Interior of Southern
   Australia, during the Years 1828, 1829, 1830 and 1831, vols I &
   II, Smith Elder & Co., London, 1833.

Wills, Dr William, A Successful Exploration through the Interior

of Australia, Friends of the State Library of South Australia,
Adelaide, 1996 (first pub. 1863).

GENERAL AUSTRALIAN EXPLORATION

Cannon, Michael, The Exploration of Australia, Reader's Digest,
Sydney, 1987.

Cumpston, J. H. L., Augustus Gregory and the Inland Sea, Angus &
Robertson, Sydney, 1965.

Favenc, Ernest, Explorers of Australia, Tiger Books International
(Senate), London, 1998.

Haynes, Roslynn D., Seeking the Centre, Cambridge University
Press, Cambridge, 1998.

Howitt, Mary, Come Wind or Weather, Melbourne University Press,
Melbourne, 1971.

McIver, George, The Drover's Odyssey, Angus & Robertson, Sydney,
1935.

Madigan, Cecil T., Central Australia, Oxford University Press,
London, 1936.

Madigan, Cecil T., Crossing the Dead Heart, Georgian House,
Melbourne, 1948.

BIOGRAPHIES AND AUTOBIOGRAPHIES

Beale, Edgar, Sturt, the Chipped Idol: A Study of Charles Sturt,
Explorer, Angus & Robertson, Sydney, 1979.

Ferguson, Charles, Experiences of a Forty-Niner during Thirty-Four
Years Residence in California and Australia, Frederick T. Wallace
(ed.), The Williams Publishing Company, Cleveland, 1888.

Lockwood, Kim, Big John: The Extraordinary Adventures of John
McKinlay, State Library of Victoria, Melbourne, 1995.

Mudie, Ian, The Heroic Journey of John McDouall Stuart, Angus &
Robertson, Sydney, 1968.

Tipping, Marjorie, Ludwig Becker: Artist and Naturalist with the Burke and Wills Expedition, Melbourne University Press, Melbourne, 1979.

Webster, Mona S., John McDouall Stuart, Melbourne University Press, Melbourne, 1958.

Young, Rose, G. F. Von Tempsky, Artist and Adventurer, Alister Taylor, Martinborough, 1981.

ABORIGINAL HISTORY

Howitt, Alfred, The Native Tribes of South-East Australia, Aboriginal Studies Press, Canberra, 1966 (first pub. 1904).

Mulvaney, D. J., The Prehistory of Australia: Ancient People and Places, Thames & Hudson, London, 1969.

Tolcher, Helen, Drought or Deluge, Melbourne University Press, Melbourne, 1986.

MONOGRAPHS, PAMPHLETS AND MAGAZINE ARTICLES

Bergin, Tom, Courage and Corruption: An Analysis of the Burke and Wills Expedition and of the Subsequent Royal Commission of Enquiry, unpublished thesis, University of New England, Armidale, 1982.

Blanchen, B. J., 'From Melbourne to Menindie: A Tourist's Guide Based on the Diaries of Ludwig Becker', La Trobe Library Journal, October 1978, pp. 34–36.

Fitzpatrick, Kathleen, 'The Burke and Wills Expedition and the Royal Society of Victoria', Historical Studies of Australia and New Zealand, 10 April 1963, pp. 470–78.

Kerwin, Bennie, and Breen, J. G., 'The Land of the Stone Chips', Oceania, vol. 51, pp. 286–311.

McKellar, John, 'John King: Sole Survivor of the Burke and Wills Expedition to the Gulf of Carpentaria', Victorian Historical Magazine, December 1944, pp. 106–9.

McKellar, John, 'William John Wills', Victorian Historical Magazine,

2 February 1962, pp. 337–50.

McLaren, Ian, 'The Victorian Exploring Expedition and Relieving Expeditions, 1860–61: The Burke and Wills Tragedy', Victorian Historical Magazine, 29 April 1959, pp. 211–53.

Threadgill, Bessie, South Australian Land Exploration, 1856 to 1880, vols I & II, Board of Governors of the Public Library, Museum, and Art Gallery of South Australia, Adelaide, 1922.

OTHER SOURCES

McKnight, Tom L., The Camel in Australia, Melbourne University Press, Melbourne, 1969.

McNicoll, Ronald, Number 36 Collins St: The Melbourne Club, Allen & Unwin, Sydney, 1988.

Rajkowski, Pamela, In the Tracks of the Camelmen: Australia's Most Exotic Pioneers, Angus & Robertson, Sydney, 1987.

Riffenburgh, Beau, The Myth of the Explorer, Oxford University Press, Oxford, 1994.

Sadleir, John, Recollections of a Victorian Police Officer, George Robertson, Melbourne, 1913.

Serle, Geoffrey, The Golden Age: A History of the Colony of Victoria, Melbourne University Press, Melbourne, 1968.

Stawell, Mary, My Recollections, Richard Clay & Sons, London, 1911.

INDEX